Amazing
MATH MAZES
ADDING AND SUBTRACTING

13 - 6

12 - 7

3 + 5

7 + 9

4 + 6

11 + 9

CATHERINE CASEY
ANA SEBASTIÁN

ARCTURUS

Arcturus

This edition published in 2024 by Arcturus Publishing Limited
26/27 Bickels Yard, 151–153 Bermondsey Street,
London SE1 3HA

Author: Catherine Casey
Illustrator: Ana Sebastián
Editor: Violet Peto
Designer: Stefan Holliland
Editorial Manager: Joe Harris

ISBN: 978-1-3988-3634-1
CH011566NT
Supplier 29, Date 0524, PI 00005859

Printed in China

HOW TO USE THIS BOOK

Welcome to the "funtastic" world of adding and subtracting mazes! This activity book is full of exciting scenes to help you learn and become confident with the basics of addition and subtraction.

Solve each equation, and then choose the correct path to reach the end.

After you have completed the maze, check that you followed the correct route by turning to pages 88-95.

Some topics come with a **Top Tip** to help you on the way.

NUMBER BONDS	10 Bonds	20 Bonds
Number bonds are pairs of numbers that make up a given number. These are some of the number bonds up to 10 and 20.	1 + 9	1 + 19
	2 + 8	2 + 18
	3 + 7	3 + 17
	4 + 6	4 + 16
	5 + 5	5 + 15

You can find a 100 square and a number line to help you on page 96.

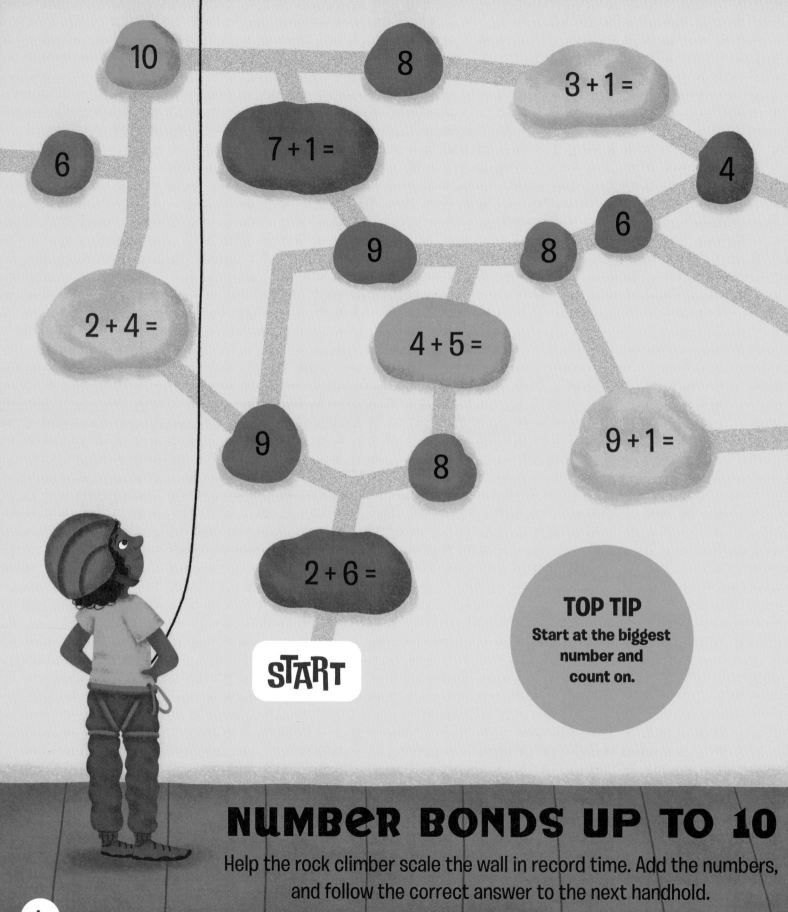

10

8

3 + 1 =

7 + 1 =

6

4

9

8

6

2 + 4 =

4 + 5 =

9

8

9 + 1 =

2 + 6 =

START

TOP TIP
Start at the biggest
number and
count on.

NUMBER BONDS UP TO 10

Help the rock climber scale the wall in record time. Add the numbers,
and follow the correct answer to the next handhold.

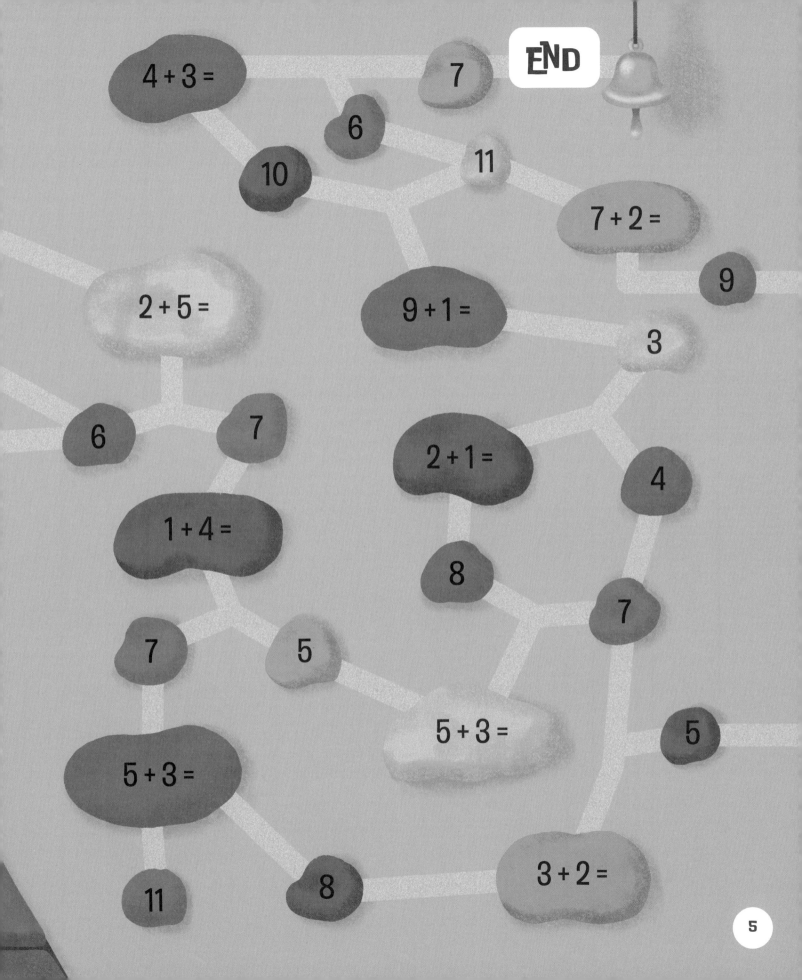

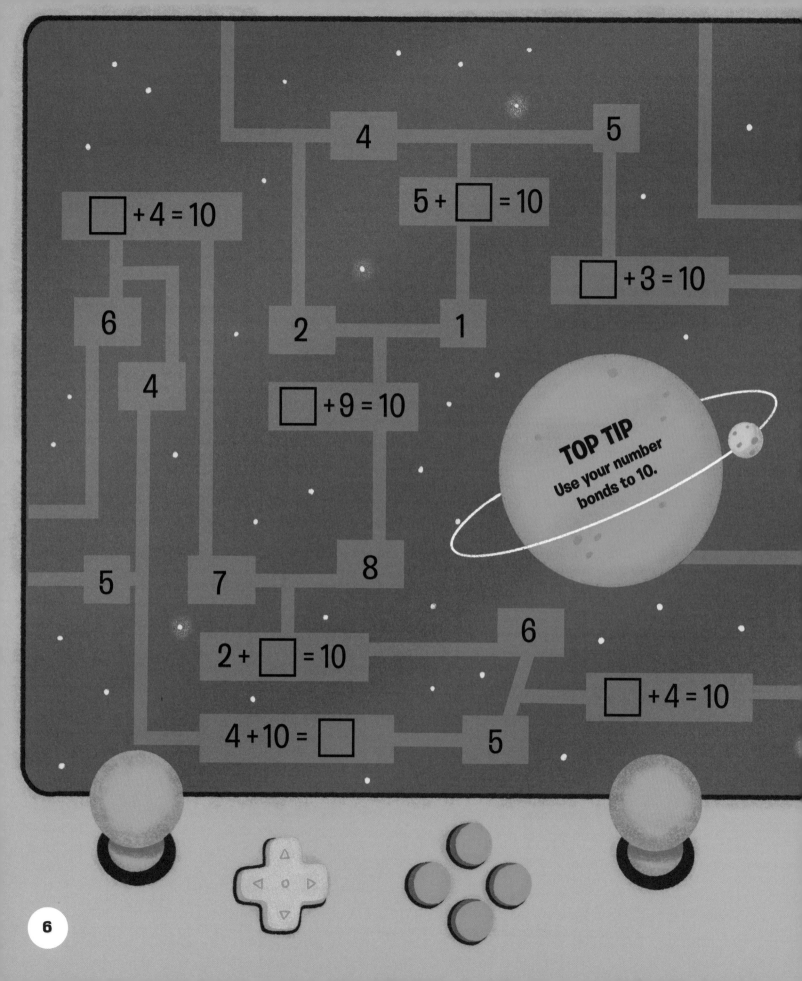

4

5

$5 + \boxed{} = 10$

$\boxed{} + 4 = 10$

$\boxed{} + 3 = 10$

6

2

1

4

$\boxed{} + 9 = 10$

TOP TIP
Use your number
bonds to 10.

8

5

7

6

$2 + \boxed{} = 10$

$\boxed{} + 4 = 10$

$4 + 10 = \boxed{}$

5

6

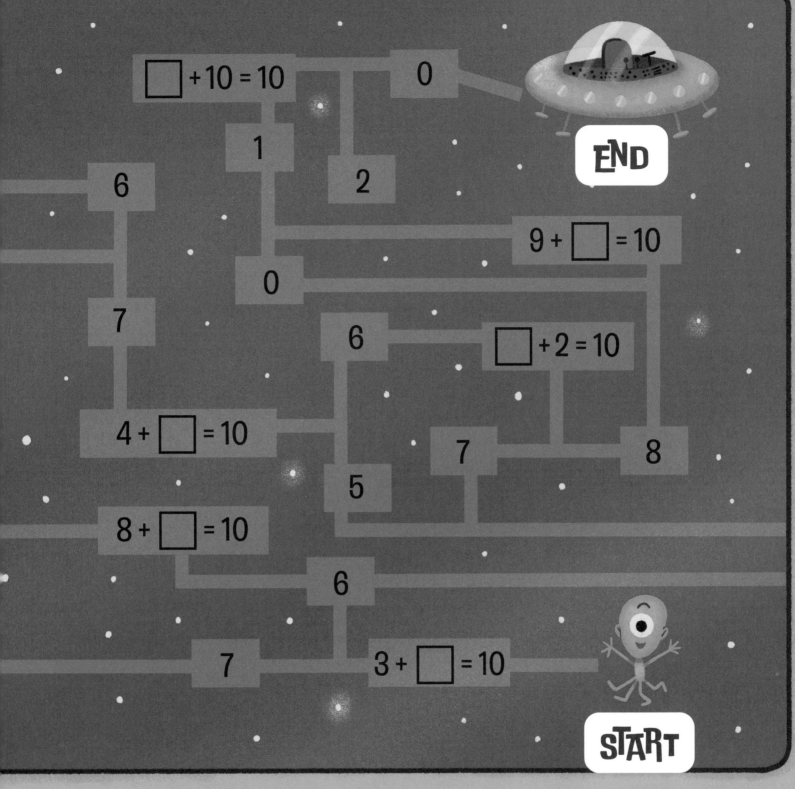

☐ + 10 = 10

0

END

1

6

2

9 + ☐ = 10

0

7

6

☐ + 2 = 10

4 + ☐ = 10

7

8

5

8 + ☐ = 10

6

7

3 + ☐ = 10

START

MAKiNG 10

Guide the computer character across the screen. Solve the
problems with the missing numbers, and follow the answers.

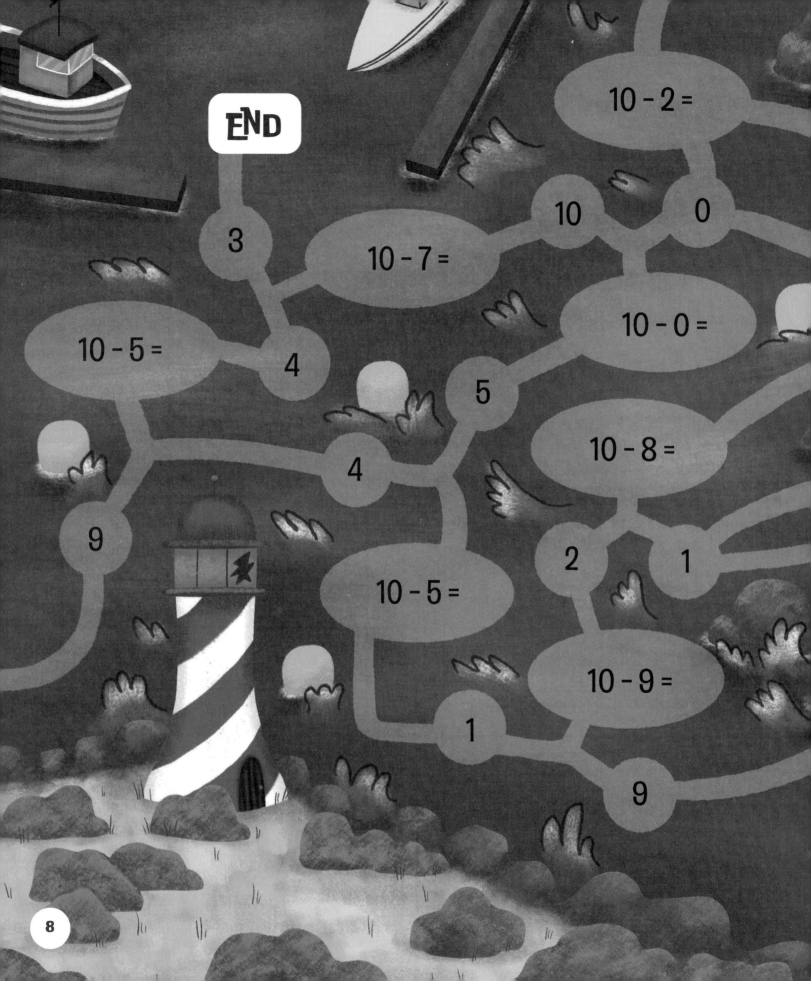

TAKE AWAY FROM 10

The lighthouse light has gone out. Can you lead the boat safely into the marina? Take away 10 from each number to avoid the rocks.

9

MISSING NUMBER PROBLEMS

Help the soccer player score the winning goal! Dodge the other players by finding the missing numbers.

$6 + \square = 9$

4

5

4

3

$\square + 3 = 8$

3

7

5

$4 + \square = 7$

$\square + 1 = 7$

6

2

8

7

$2 + \square = 5$

3

$\square + 2 = 9$

START

1

7

6

$5 + \boxed{} = 6$

$\boxed{} + 3 = 9$

$\boxed{} + 5 = 8$

3

8

3

$\boxed{} + 2 = 4$

2

END

$\boxed{} + 1 = 8$

0

6

7

5

$\boxed{} + 10 = 10$

$4 + \boxed{} = 9$

9

5

$5 + \boxed{} = 10$

11

ADDING 10

Help the worm wiggle its way to the surface.
Add 10 to each number to choose the correct route!

0+10=

10

5+10

25

START

100

15

10+10=

6+10

3

20

14

13

3+10=

13

4+10

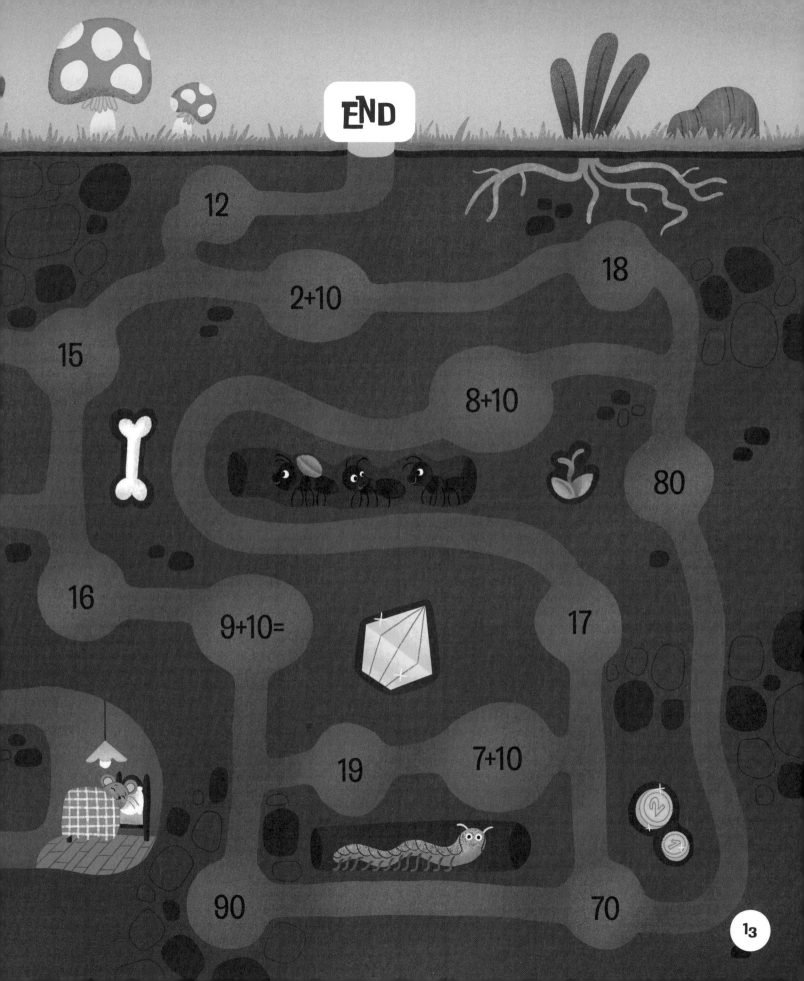

NUMBERS UP TO 20

Help the polar bear hop over the icebergs back to her cub. Add the numbers, and follow the correct answer to find the next iceberg.

END

20

15 + 2 =

19

16 + 3 =

14

15

TOP TIP
Use your number bonds
to help you.
2 + 5 = 7
2 + 15 = 17

2 + 12 =

8 + 11 =

13

20

19

4 + 9 =

14

11

18

5 + 13 =

4 + 7 =

19

4 + 9 =

15

12

9

13

6 + ☐ = 20

7 + ☐ = 20

12

15

10 + ☐ = 20

14

10

6 + ☐ = 20

0

END

18

19

2 + ☐ = 20

9

11

1 + ☐ = 20

5

15 + ☐ = 20

4

MAKING 20

Fly the bird back to her nest. Solve the problems with the missing numbers, and find the correct route through the trees.

7

$12 + \boxed{} = 20$

START

8

$17 + \boxed{} = 20$

3

4   3 $16 + \boxed{} = 20$

4

$11 + \boxed{} = 20$

$11 + \boxed{} = 20$

3          $18 + \boxed{} = 20$ 9   10

2

TAKE AWAY FROM 20

Zoom through outer space, and land on the moon.
Take away the numbers from 20, and whoosh
along the correct route.

END

10

20

20 - 0 =

20 - 1 =

11

20

20 - 6 =

15

14

19

20 - 10 =

20 - 1 =

18

17

START

20 - 3 =

18

20 - 7 =

12

13

13

12

20 - 8 =

TOP TIP
Start at 20 and
count back.

20 - 9 =

16

15

12

11

20 - 4 =

20 - 2 =

16

15

17

18

20 - 5 =

20 - 5 =

5

MISSING NUMBER PROBLEMS

Beep beep! Help the robot sort the packages in the warehouse.
Find the missing numbers to guide you to the package.

START

END

3

$16 - \square = 12$

$16 - \square = 11$

4

$17 - \square = 12$

9

11

4

5

$12 - \square = 4$

5

8

9

8

$15 - \square = 10$

$12 - \square = 3$

9

7

4

5

$13 - \square = 6$

20

11 − ☐ = 3

4   8   3   2

12 − ☐ = 3

20 − ☐ = 14   14 − ☐ = 11

6   4

9

10

TOP TIP
Use a number line to
count back.

6   19 − ☐ = 10

9   16

18 − ☐ = 12

3   16 − ☐ = 9

8

15 − ☐ = 8   7

START

$3 + 3 =$

7

6

$7 + 7 =$

14

$1 + 1 =$

3

TOP TIP
Doubling means two of the same
number added together.
Double 4 = 4 + 4

11

2

11

$4 + 4 =$

8

$5 + 5 =$

7

$4 + 4 =$

10

2 + 2 =

6

5 + 5 =

12

4

20

10 + 10 =

8 + 8 =

16

10

17

1 + 1 =

9 + 9 =

14

12

6 + 6 =

12

END

8

DOUBLES

Race the go-kart to the finish line. Double the numbers to stay on the right track. Watch out for cones blocking your path. On your marks, get set, GO!

MORE DOUBLES

Help the frog hop over the lily pads to get across the pond. Double the numbers to hop onto the correct lily pad each time.

START

TOP TIP
Doubling means two of the same number added together.
Double 12 = 12 + 12

11 + 11 =

23

22

12 + 12 =

16 + 16 =

24

25

26

35

13 + 13 =

27

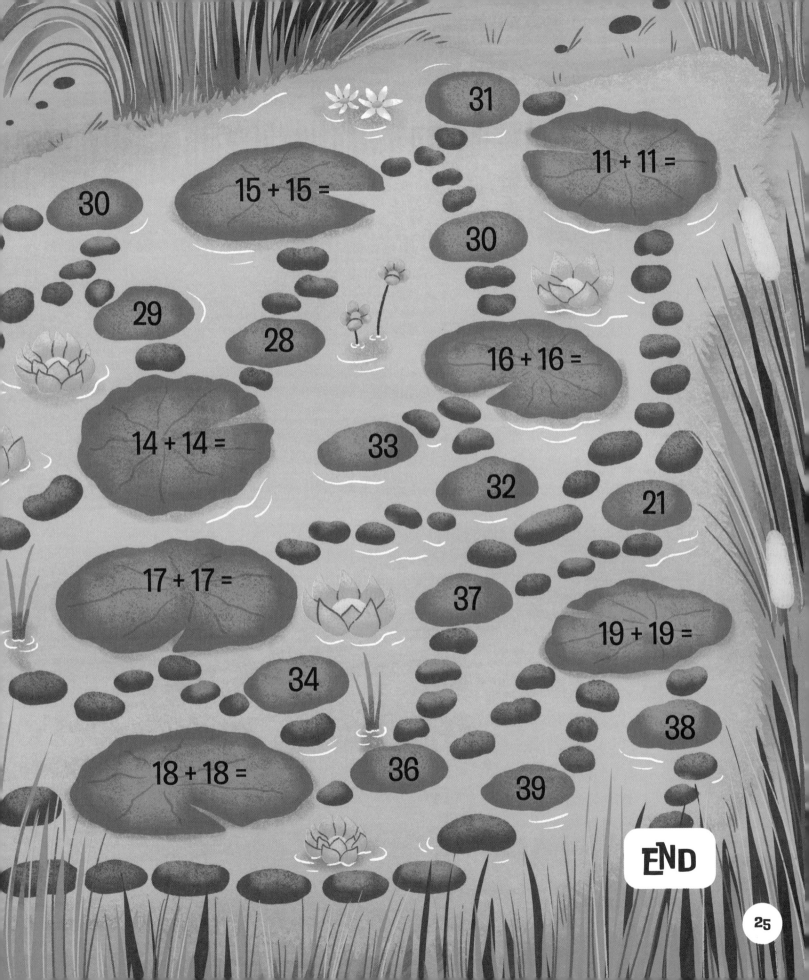

ADDING A ONE-DIGIT NUMBER

It's your job to guide the plane safely down to the runway. Add the one-digit number to the two-digit number, and follow the correct answers.

START

$23 + 4 =$

28

$6 + 32 =$

27

28

$27 + 1 =$

29

38

39

$23 + 5 =$

45

$41 + 5 =$

46

TOP TIP

Add the ones and then the tens.

44 + 3 =

47

48

2 + 26 =

37

16 + 3 =

38

38

5 + 34 =

28

33 + 4 =

30

8 + 21 =

38

39

29

1 + 46 =

15 + 2 =

48

47

END

ADDING MULTIPLES OF 10

Take the alpaca for a walk around the mountains. Add the multiples of 10 to follow the correct path.

60 + 30 =

5

20 + 30 =

10 + 30 =

50

START

10 + 50 =

40

50

70

60

TOP TIP

Use your number bonds
and place values to help.
3 + 4 = 7
30 + 40 = 70

40 + 20 =

70

80 + 10 =

60

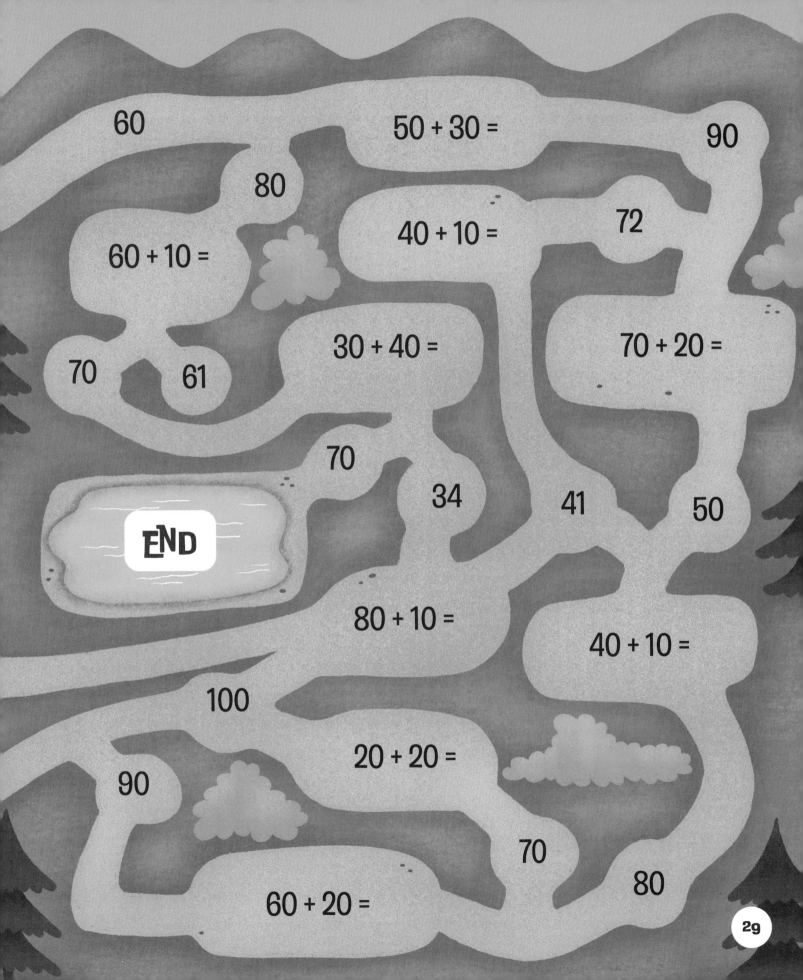

60

50 + 30 =

90

80

60 + 10 =

40 + 10 =

72

70

61

30 + 40 =

70 + 20 =

70

34

41

50

END

80 + 10 =

40 + 10 =

100

20 + 20 =

90

70

80

60 + 20 =

START

18 + 10 =

28

19

42

51

64 + 10 =

23 + 10 =

73

74

42

52

47

37 + 10 =

48

37 + 10 =

END

ADDING 10 TO A TWO-DIGIT NUMBER

This pirate is seeking the treasure. Can you get there first? Add 10 to each two-digit number to find the way to the treasure.

27 + 10 =

37

71 + 10 =

17

81

710

41 + 10 =

54

44 + 10 =

45

13

62 + 10 =

33

32 + 10 =

66

56 + 10 =

TOP TIP
Use a hundred
square to help you.

89 + 10 =

46

79

99

ADDING MULTIPLES OF TEN

Guide the mountain biker down the twists and turns of this trail. Add multiples of 10 to each two-digit number to show the way.

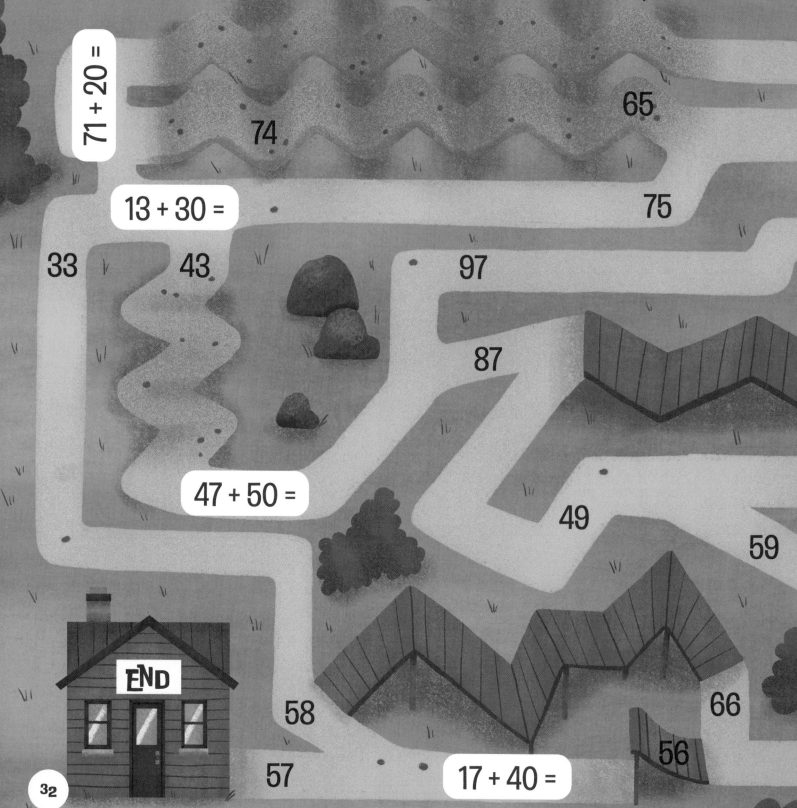

71 + 20 =

65

74

13 + 30 =

75

33

43

97

87

47 + 50 =

49

59

END

58

66

56

57

17 + 40 =

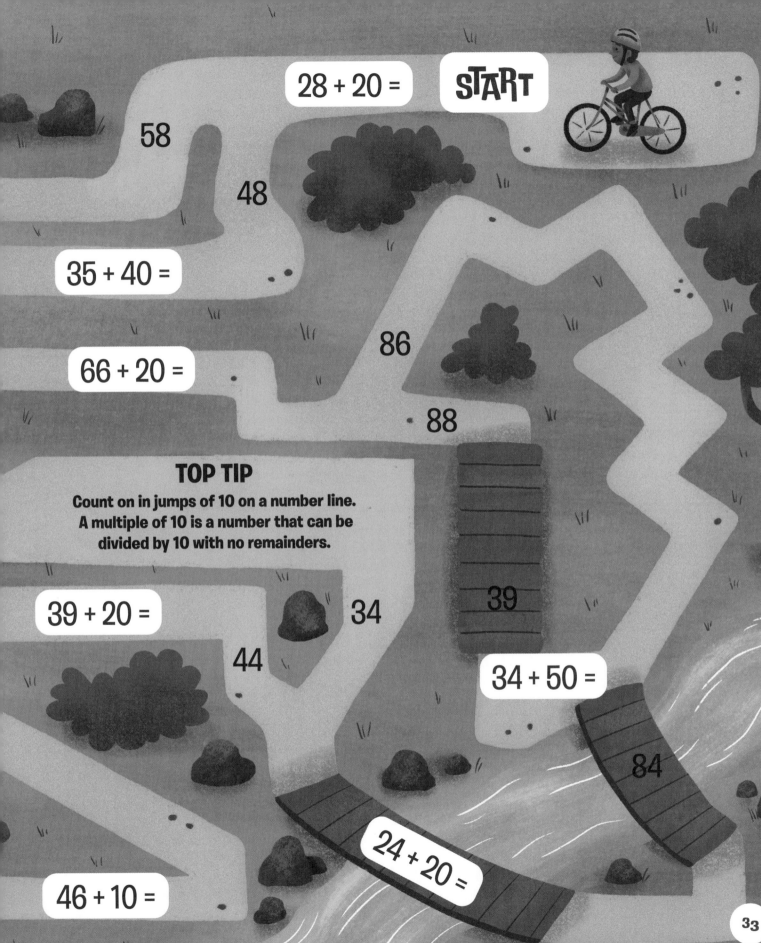

28 + 20 =

START

58

48

35 + 40 =

86

66 + 20 =

88

TOP TIP

Count on in jumps of 10 on a number line.
A multiple of 10 is a number that can be
divided by 10 with no remainders.

39

39 + 20 =

34

44

34 + 50 =

46 + 10 =

84

24 + 20 =

35 + 22 =

57

54

24 + 33 =

85

86

64 + 21 =

END

73

54

41 + 32 =

22 + 47 =

88

62 + 15 =

96

69

78

67

77

56 + 21 =

34

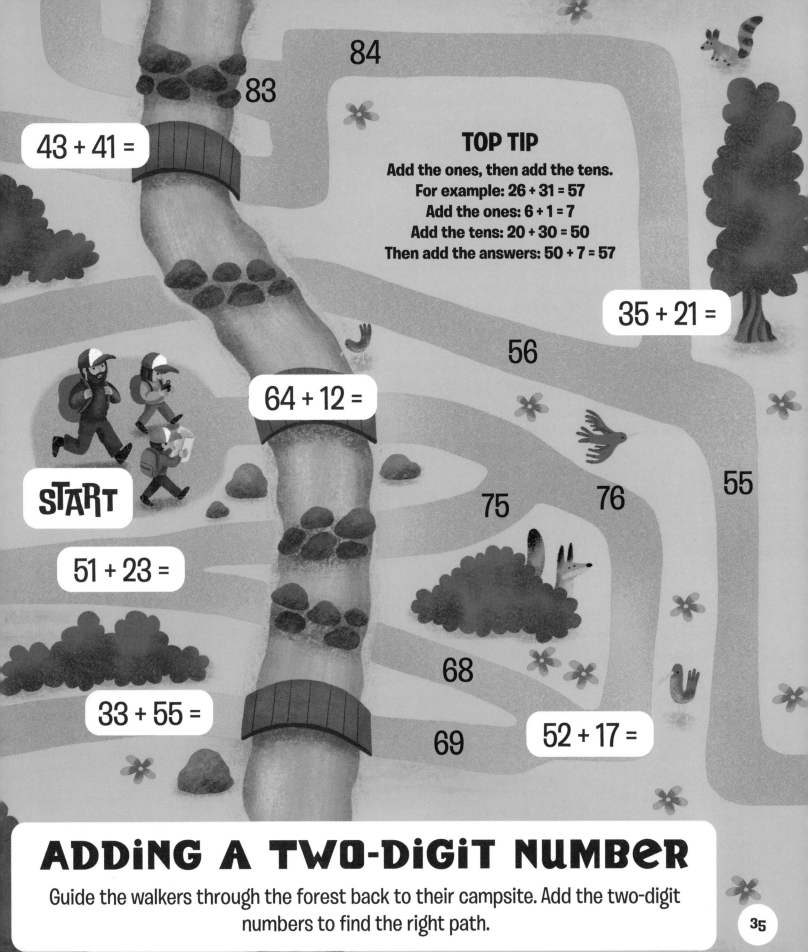

84

83

43 + 41 =

TOP TIP
Add the ones, then add the tens.
For example: 26 + 31 = 57
Add the ones: 6 + 1 = 7
Add the tens: 20 + 30 = 50
Then add the answers: 50 + 7 = 57

35 + 21 =

56

64 + 12 =

55

START

75   76

51 + 23 =

33 + 55 =

68

69   52 + 17 =

ADDING A TWO-DIGIT NUMBER

Guide the walkers through the forest back to their campsite. Add the two-digit numbers to find the right path.

ADD THREE NUMBERS

Speed around the aisles to the checkout. Don't knock anything over on the way! Add three numbers together to choose the quickest route.

15

6 + 6 + 1 =

9 + 4 + 1 =

14

16

14

2 + 8 + 6 =

13

15

TOP TIP
Look for doubles or number bonds.

5 + 5 + 3 =

11

1 + 3 + 7 =

10

START

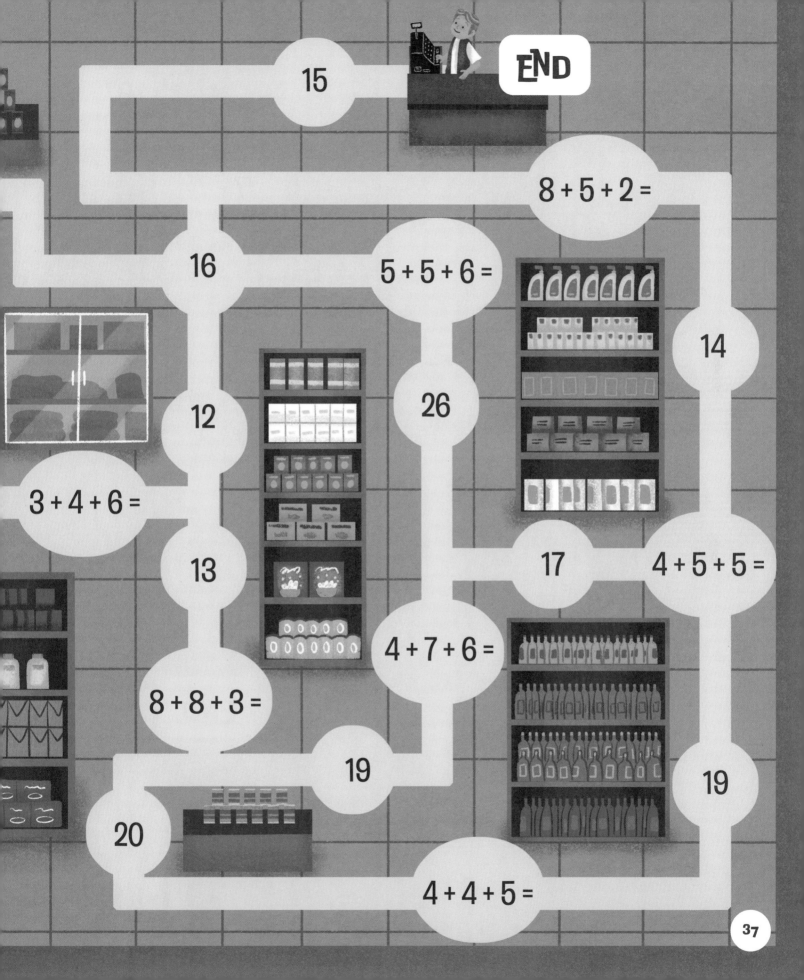

15

END

8 + 5 + 2 =

16

5 + 5 + 6 =

14

12

26

3 + 4 + 6 =

17

4 + 5 + 5 =

13

4 + 7 + 6 =

8 + 8 + 3 =

19

19

20

4 + 4 + 5 =

37

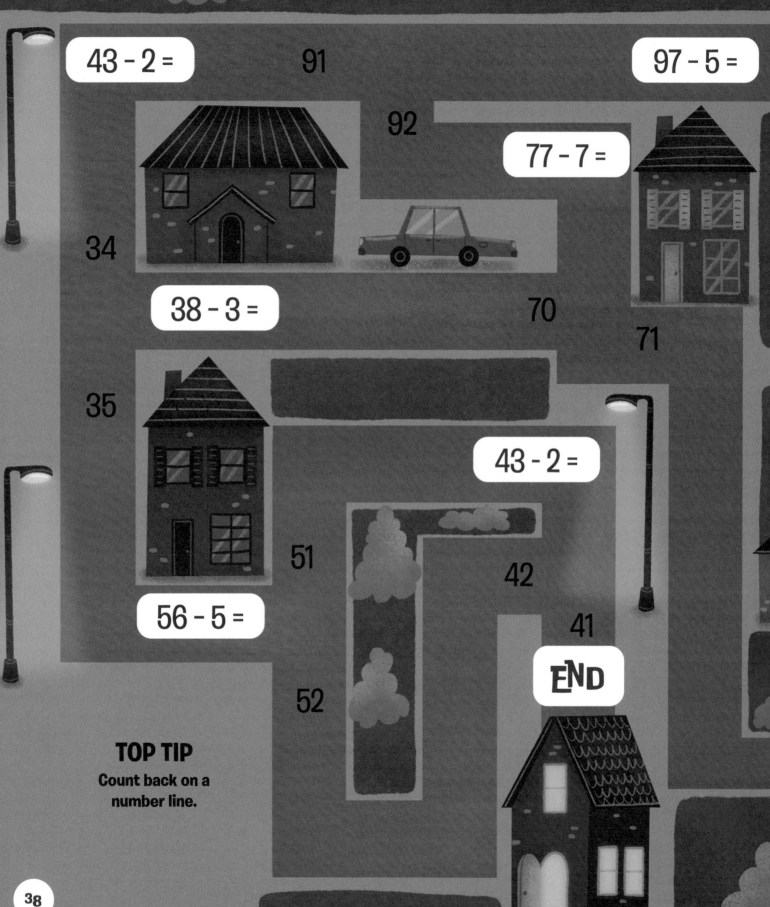

43 − 2 =

91

97 − 5 =

92

77 − 7 =

34

38 − 3 =

70

71

35

43 − 2 =

51

42

56 − 5 =

41

END

52

TOP TIP
Count back on a
number line.

38

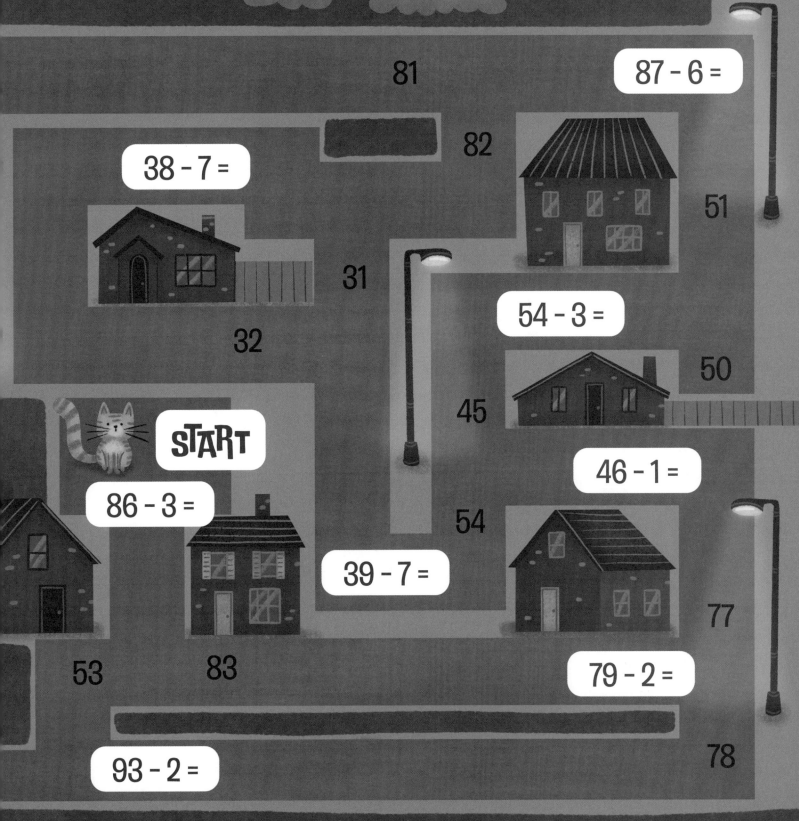

81

87 - 6 =

38 - 7 =

82

51

31

54 - 3 =

32

50

START

45

86 - 3 =

46 - 1 =

54

39 - 7 =

77

53   83

79 - 2 =

93 - 2 =

78

TAKE AWAY A ONE-DIGIT NUMBER

Show this little cat the way back home. Take away the one-digit from the
two-digit number to find the correct house.

TAKE AWAY 10

Help the dinosaur back to her eggs before they hatch! Take away 10 from each two-digit number to get her through the volcanic landscape.

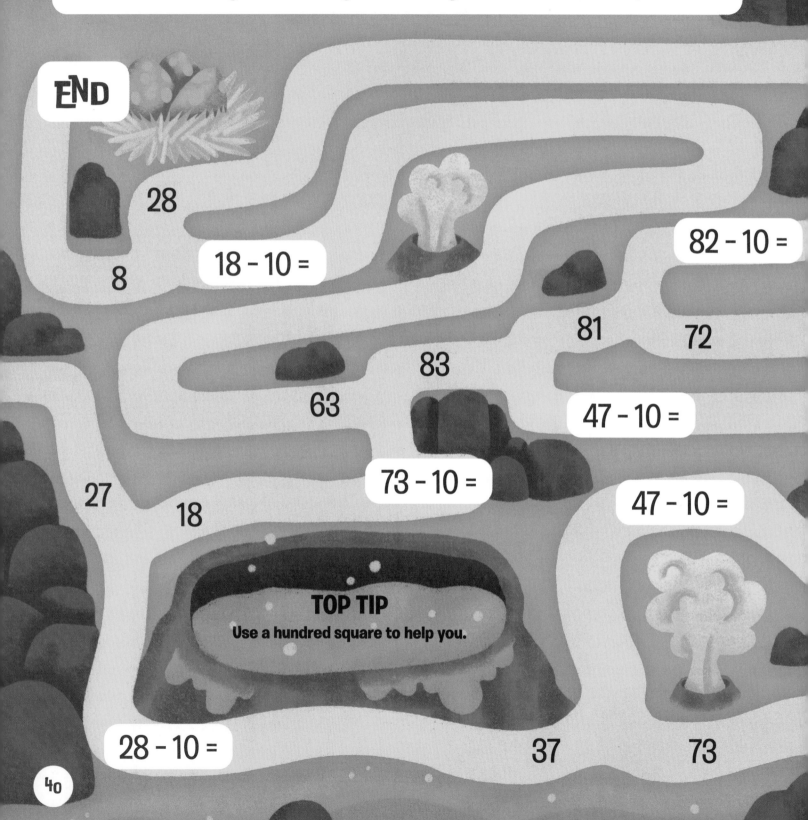

END

28

8

18 - 10 =

82 - 10 =

81

72

83

63

47 - 10 =

73 - 10 =

47 - 10 =

27

18

TOP TIP

Use a hundred square to help you.

28 - 10 =

37

73

START

$56 - 10 =$

$45 - 10 =$

46

55

$64 - 10 =$

54

44

21

$31 - 10 =$

30

$45 - 10 =$

33

$98 - 10 =$

35

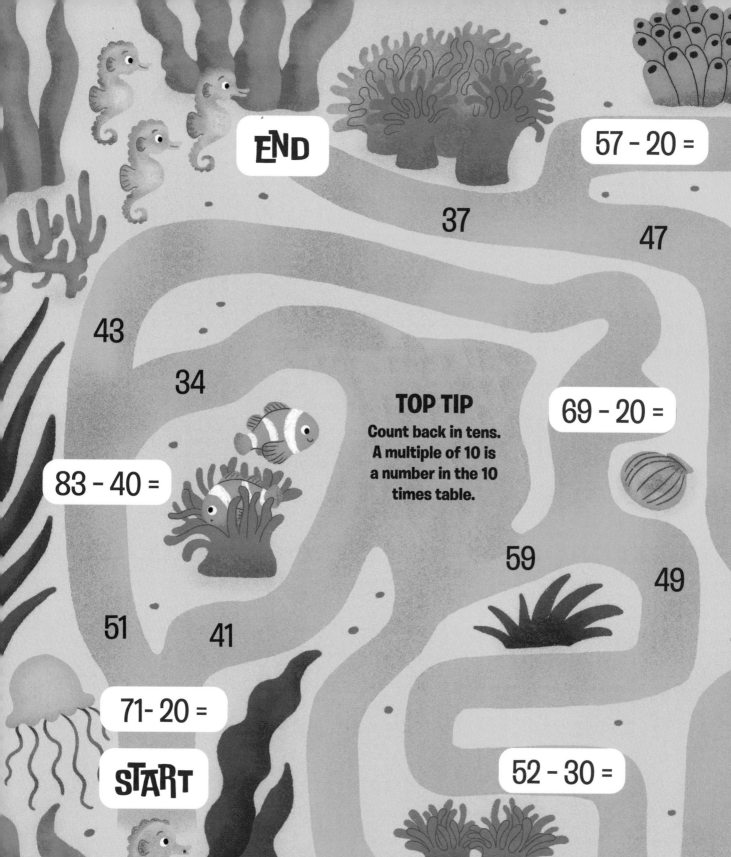

END

57 - 20 =

37

47

43

34

TOP TIP
Count back in tens.
A multiple of 10 is
a number in the 10
times table.

69 - 20 =

83 - 40 =

59

49

51

41

71 - 20 =

START

52 - 30 =

32

22

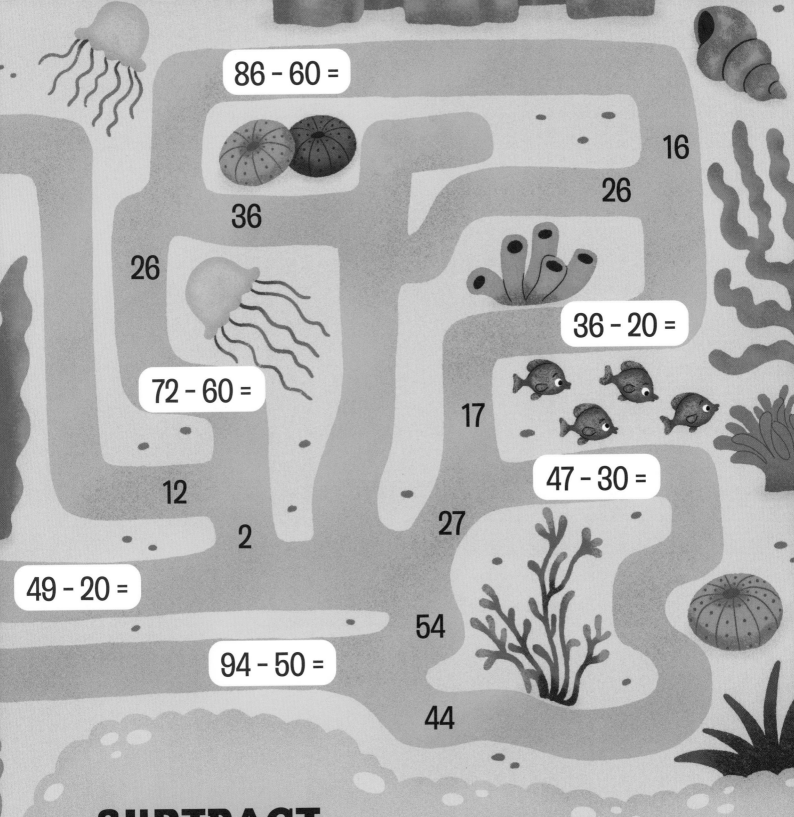

86 - 60 =

16

26

36

26

72 - 60 =

36 - 20 =

17

47 - 30 =

12

2

27

49 - 20 =

54

94 - 50 =

44

SUBTRACT A MULTIPLE OF 10

Guide the seahorse through the coral back to his friends. Take away the multiple of 10 to find the correct way to travel.

TAKE AWAY A TWO-DIGIT NUMBER

Help the snail slither his way to the lettuce. Take away the two-digit numbers to learn which way to go next.

31

72 – 41 =

63 – 12 =

32

54

58 – 13 =

45

27 – 16 =

53 – 24 =

12

33

11

34

END

55 – 21 =

START

$59 - 32 =$

27   72

$67 - 42 =$

15

25

$46 - 25 =$

21

31

$85 - 63 =$

24

22

TOP TIP

Take away the ones. Then take away the tens.

27

28

$39 - 12 =$

21

$96 - 65 =$

31

24 + 24 =

46

23 + 23 =

45

47

48

43   44

25 + 25 =

TOP TIP
Double the tens and
double the ones.

13 + 13 =

22 + 22 =

51   53

50

54

26 + 26 =

52   51

27 + 27 =

DOUBLES TO 30

Will you help the penguin waddle down for a swim in the sea? Double the numbers and follow the answers for the correct route.

DOUBLES TO 50

Dribble the ball, dodge the other players, and dunk into the hoop. Double the numbers to dribble along the correct path.

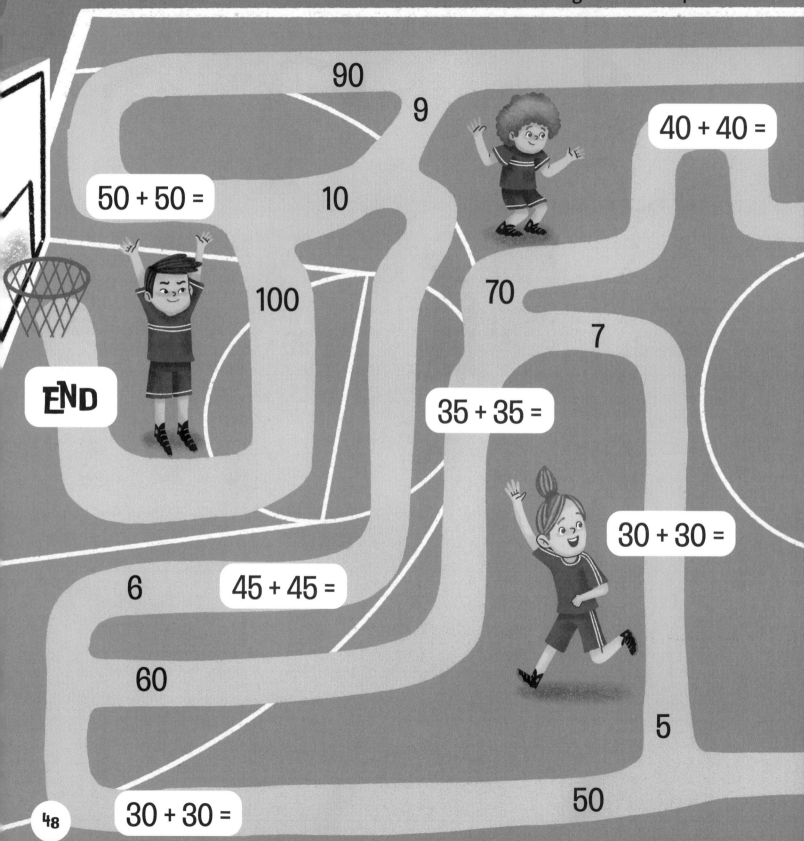

90

9

40 + 40 =

50 + 50 =

10

100

70

7

END

35 + 35 =

30 + 30 =

6

45 + 45 =

60

5

50

30 + 30 =

45 + 45 =

45 + 45 =

80

2

20

8

10 + 10 =

15 + 15 =

START

30

3

20 + 20 =

25 + 25 =

4

40

25 + 25 =

TOP TIP
Remember
$5 + 5 = 10$

DOUBLES TO 100

Race the runner to the finish line. Ready steady GO! Double the numbers to direct you along the route.

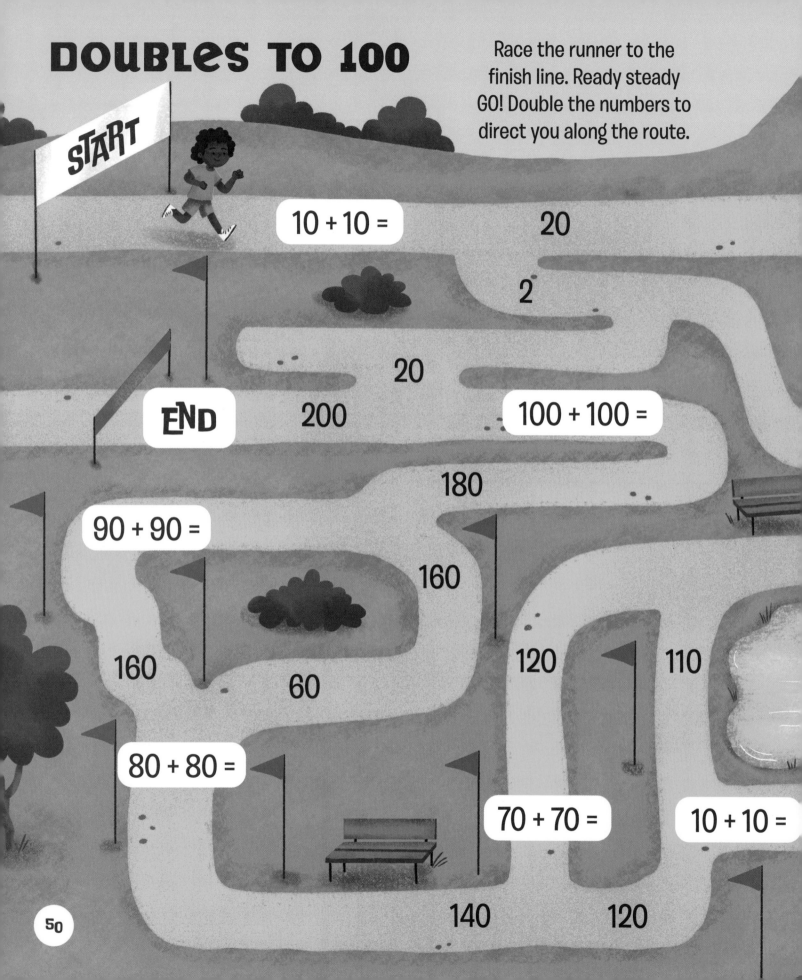

START

10 + 10 =

20

2

20

END

200

100 + 100 =

180

90 + 90 =

160

160

120

110

60

80 + 80 =

70 + 70 =

10 + 10 =

140

120

50

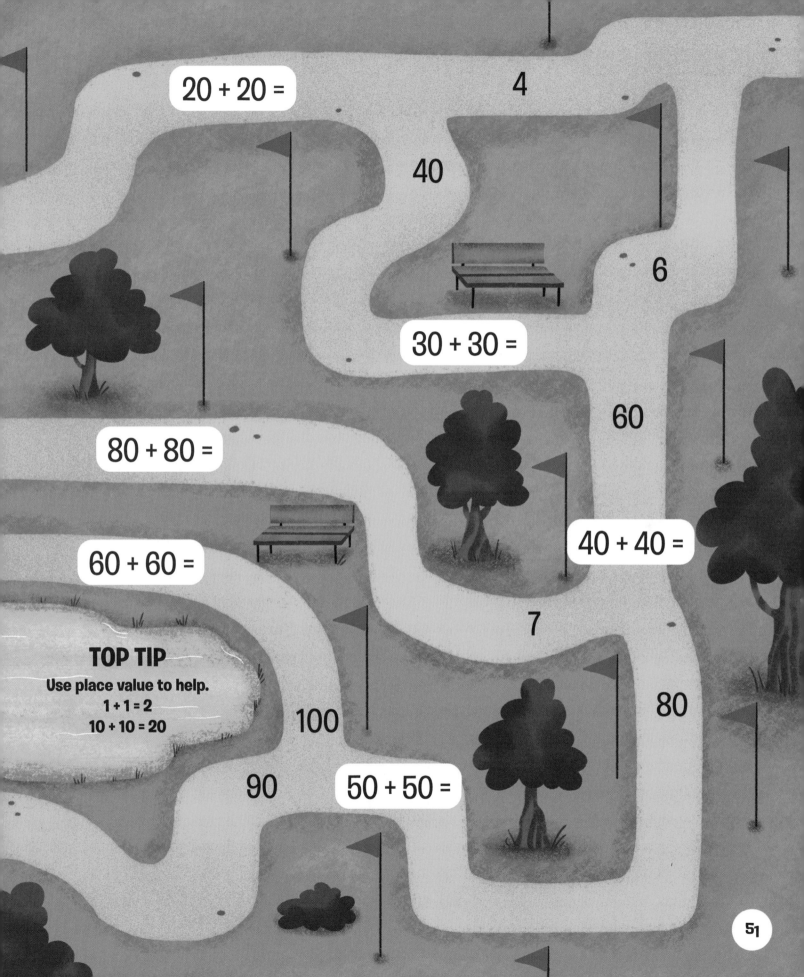

20 + 20 =

4

40

30 + 30 =

6

80 + 80 =

60

60 + 60 =

40 + 40 =

TOP TIP
Use place value to help.
1 + 1 = 2
10 + 10 = 20

7

100

80

90

50 + 50 =

ADD THREE MULTIPLES OF 10

The mouse is out of his house and hunting for the cheese! Add the three multiples of 10 to find the way to the cheese. Watch out for the cat along the way.

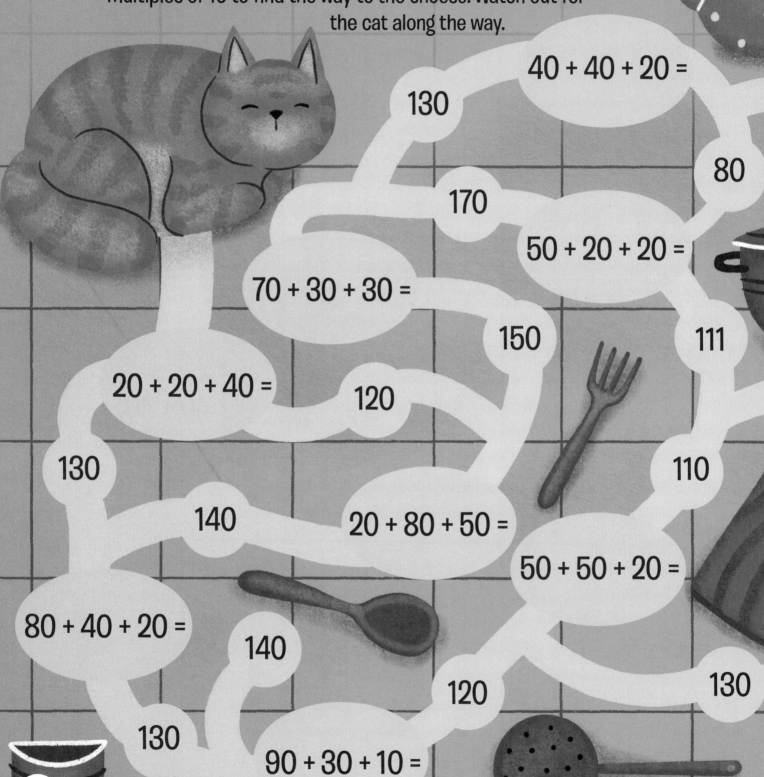

$40 + 40 + 20 =$

130

170

80

$50 + 20 + 20 =$

$70 + 30 + 30 =$

150

111

$20 + 20 + 40 =$

120

130

110

140

$20 + 80 + 50 =$

$50 + 50 + 20 =$

$80 + 40 + 20 =$

140

130

120

130

$90 + 30 + 10 =$

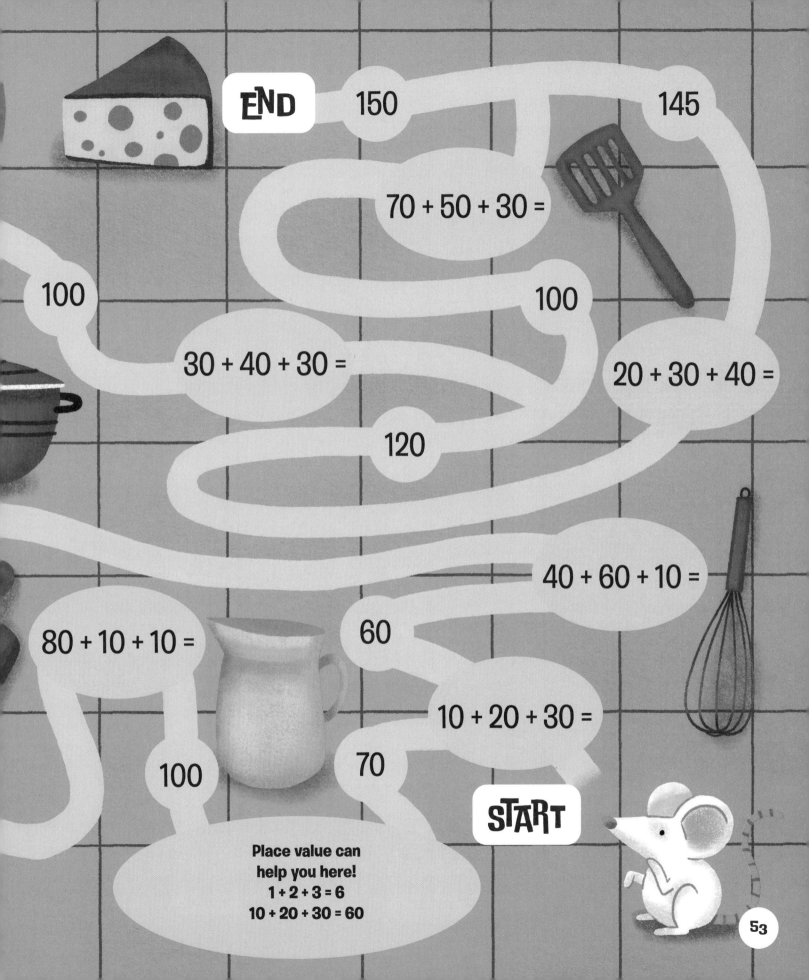

END

150

145

70 + 50 + 30 =

100

100

30 + 40 + 30 =

20 + 30 + 40 =

120

40 + 60 + 10 =

80 + 10 + 10 =

60

10 + 20 + 30 =

100

70

START

Place value can
help you here!
1 + 2 + 3 = 6
10 + 20 + 30 = 60

FIND THE MISSING NUMBERS

The train is chugging along the track back to the station. Fill in the missing numbers and follow the answer to signal the train in the right direction.

20

$74 + \boxed{} = 94$

50

$97 - \boxed{} = 17$

$82 - \boxed{} = 32$

20

$36 + \boxed{} = 56$

40

40

$29 + \boxed{} = 59$

50

$12 + \boxed{} = 62$

50

$15 + \boxed{} = 55$

30

10

START

$27 - \boxed{} = 17$

20

$48 + \boxed{} = 68$

30

TOP TIP
Check if the calculation is addition or subtraction!

20   30

90

40

$83 - \boxed{} = 43$

80

40

$61 - \boxed{} = 31$

30

END

$76 - \boxed{} = 46$

20

$45 + \boxed{} = 65$

30

$31 + \boxed{} = 61$

ONE MORE

The busy bee is buzzing from flower to flower. Guide her round the garden back to her hive. Add one to find the next flower and the bee hive.

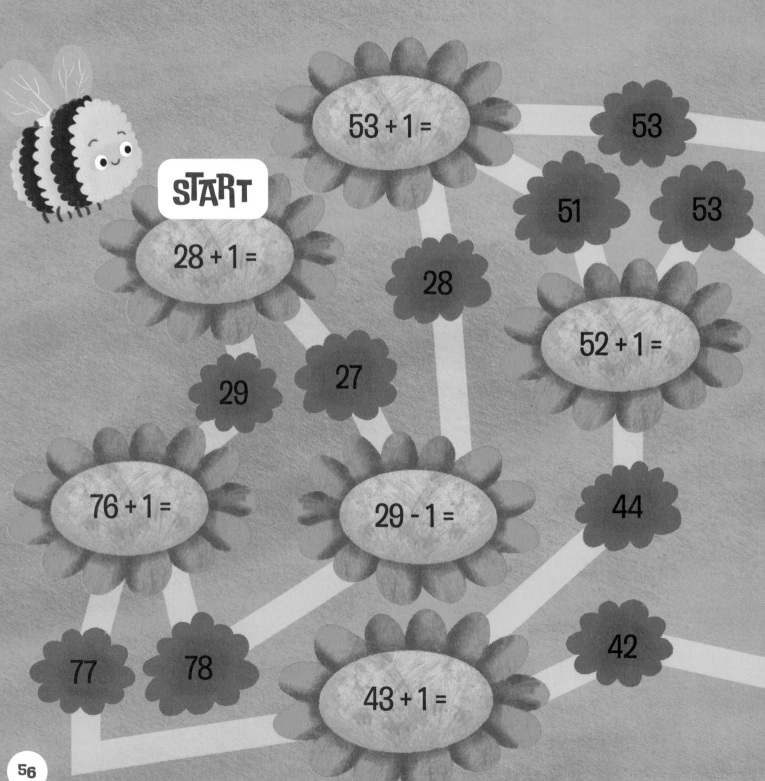

START

53 + 1 =

53

28 + 1 =

51

53

28

52 + 1 =

29

27

76 + 1 =

29 - 1 =

44

42

77

78

43 + 1 =

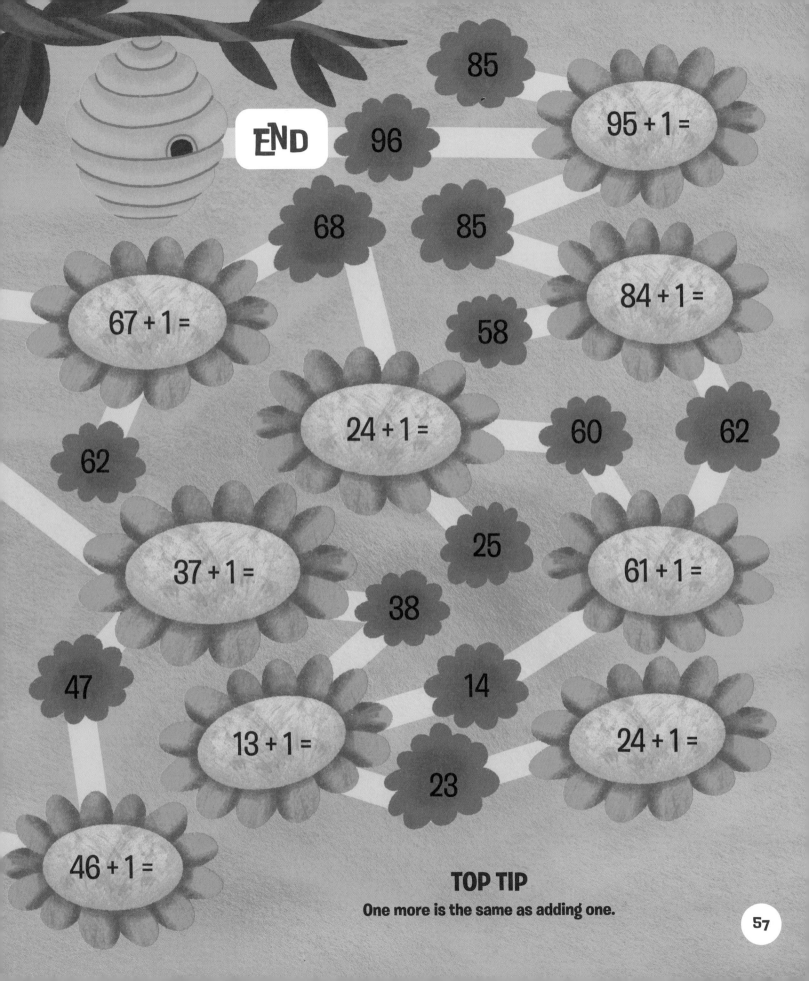

85

END

96

95 + 1 =

68

85

67 + 1 =

84 + 1 =

58

62

24 + 1 =

60

62

37 + 1 =

25

61 + 1 =

38

47

14

13 + 1 =

24 + 1 =

23

46 + 1 =

TOP TIP

One more is the same as adding one.

57

ONe Less

Help the butterfly follow the sweet scent of delicious fruits. Take-away one and follow the path.

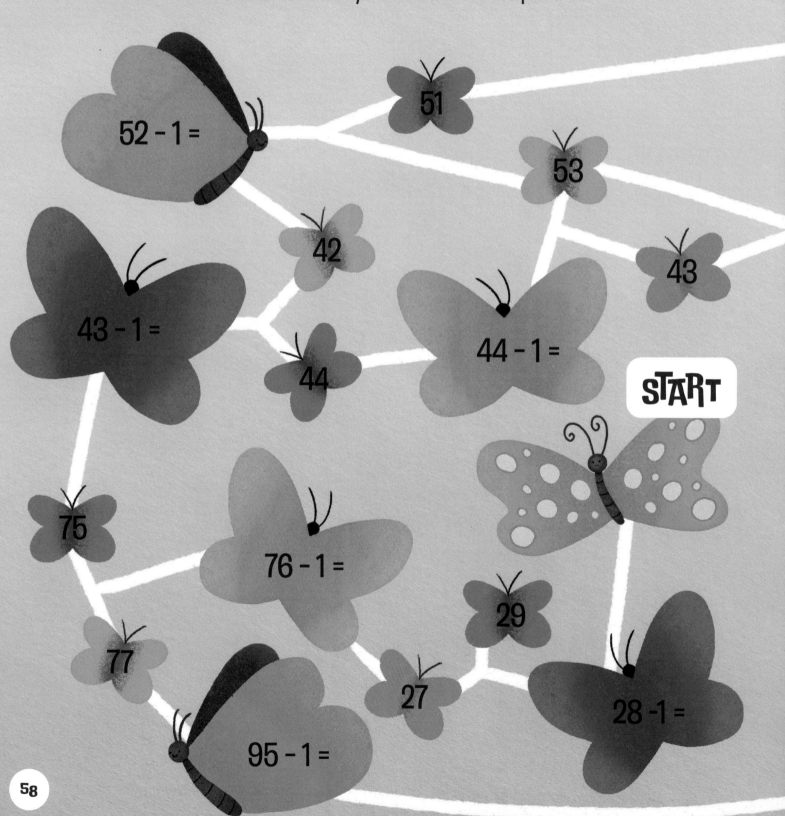

51

53

52 - 1 =

42

43

43 - 1 =

44 - 1 =

44

START

75

76 - 1 =

29

77

27

28 -1 =

95 - 1 =

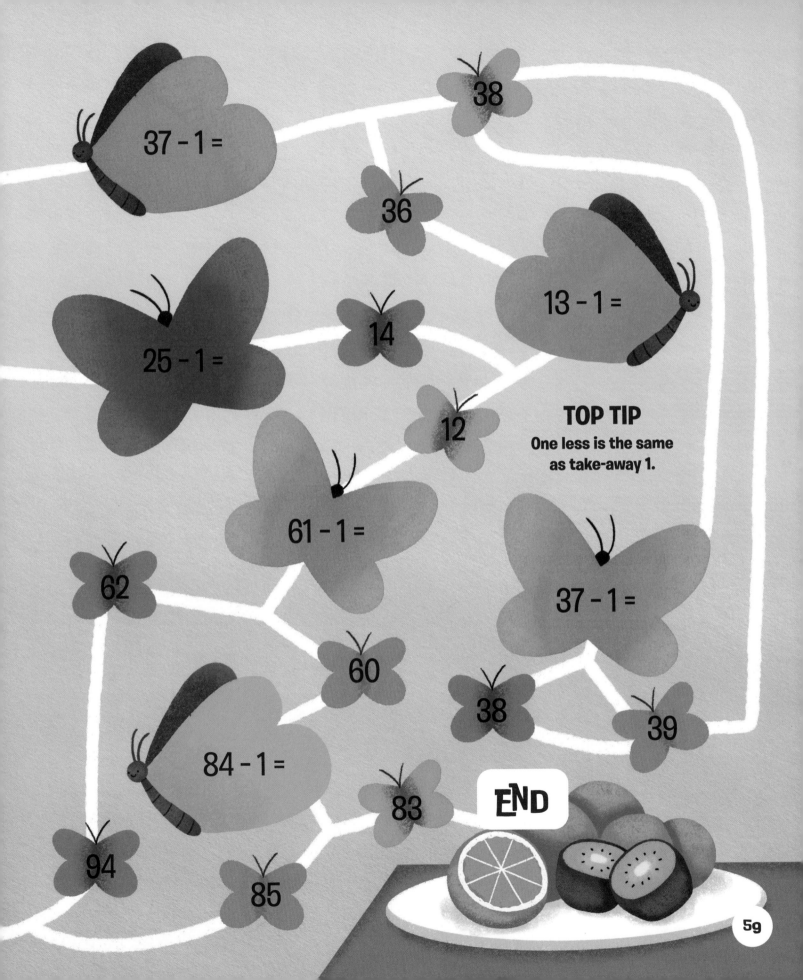

38

37 − 1 =

36

25 − 1 =

14

13 − 1 =

12

TOP TIP
One less is the same
as take-away 1.

61 − 1 =

62

37 − 1 =

60

84 − 1 =

38

39

83

END

94

85

59

ADDING 1

Binoculars at the ready! This explorer is searching for a rare parrot. Add one to journey through the jungle.

START

9 + 1 =

19

29 + 1 =

10

58

18

19 + 1 =

20

60

59 + 1 =

79 + 1 =

70

69 + 1 =

60

99 + 1 =

39 + 1 =

TOP TIP
One more is the
same as adding one.

28

30

40

30

29 + 1 =

49 + 1 =

40

50

59 + 1 =

80

70

89 + 1 =

60

100

90

END

SUBTRACTING ONE

The truck is delivering parcels. Take-away one and follow the answers around the road to the correct house.

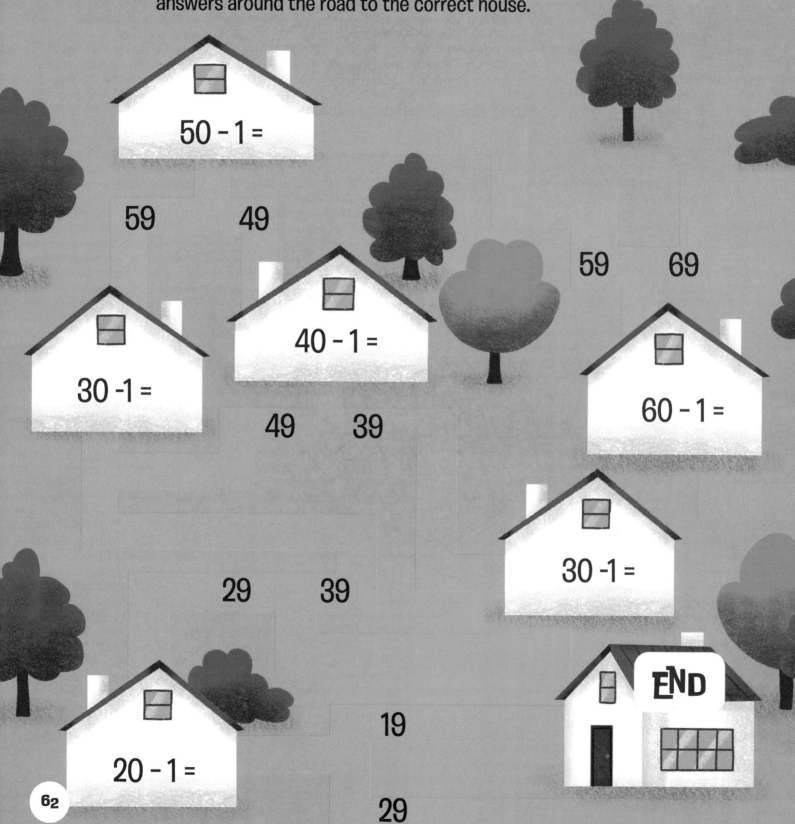

50 - 1 =

59   49

59   69

30 - 1 =

40 - 1 =

60 - 1 =

49   39

30 - 1 =

29   39

19

20 - 1 =

END

29

100 - 1 =

109   99

START

90 - 1 =

80 - 1 =

99   89

TOP TIP
One less is the same
as take-away one.

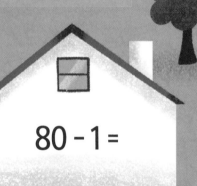

80 - 1 =

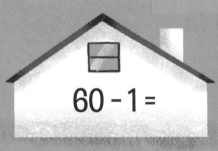

60 - 1 =

69   71

89

79

70 - 1 =

63

ADDING A 1-DIGIT NUMBER ACROSS THE 10S

Can you get across the busy beach to the ice-cream van? Add the 1-digit numbers to the 2-digit numbers to complete each problem.

$2 + 79 =$

$2 + 88 =$

61

63

90

$7 + 65 =$

91

$9 + 52 =$

END

72

$6 + 38 =$

32

33

71

$4 + 28 =$

81

$4 + 37 =$

82

$3 + 79 =$

64

81

START

5 + 26 =

31

30

6 + 55 =

7 + 24 =

60

61

TOP TIP

Start with the bigger number and count on.

31

8 + 34 =

9 + 63 =

33

42

43

7 + 46 =

52

71

72

53

START

100 + 23 =

100 + 37 =

115

114

100 + 15 =

174

123

231

175

100 + 82 =

182

281

100 + 74 =

66

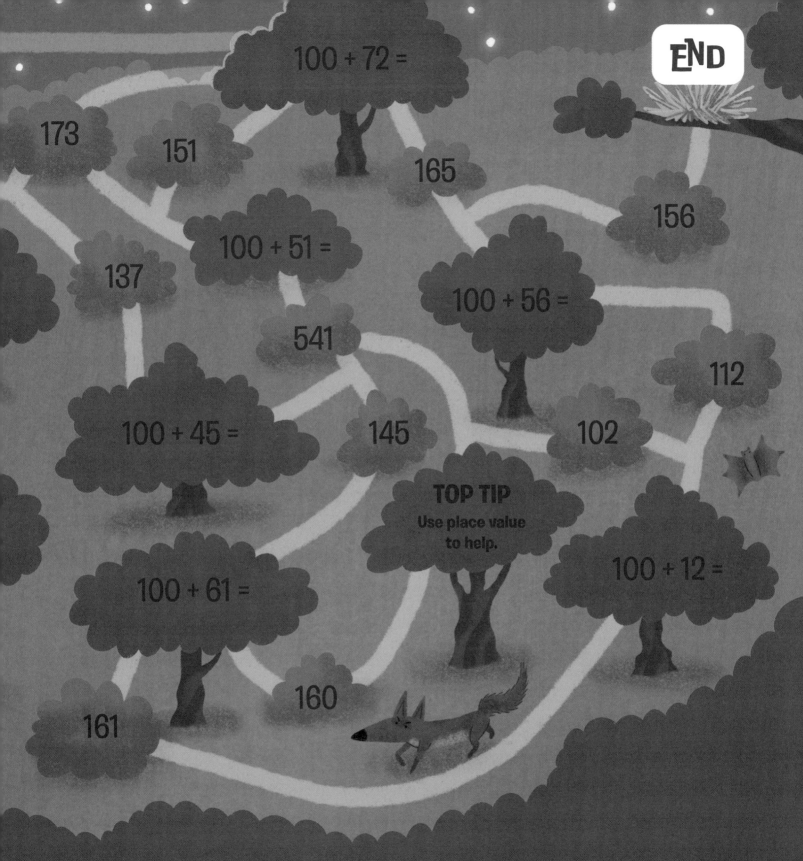

END

100 + 72 =

173

151

165

156

100 + 51 =

137

100 + 56 =

541

112

100 + 45 =

145

102

TOP TIP
Use place value
to help.

100 + 61 =

100 + 12 =

161

160

ADDING 100

Fly the owl through the night sky back to her nest.
Add 100 to each 2-digit number and follow the
correct answer.

END

53

70 + 29 =

43

89

30 + 23 =

99

62

40 + 48 =

63

61

80 + 13 =

40 + 22 =

60 + 14 =

93

92

55

65

60 + 14 =

20 + 35 =

74

75

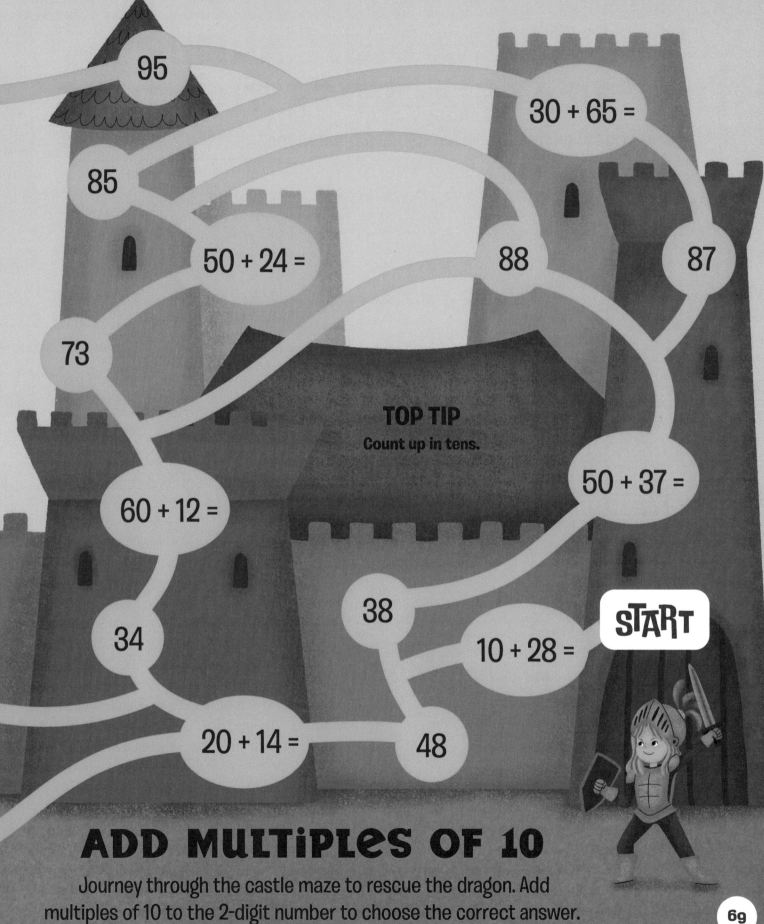

95

30 + 65 =

85

50 + 24 =

88

87

73

TOP TIP
Count up in tens.

50 + 37 =

60 + 12 =

38

START

34

10 + 28 =

20 + 14 =

48

ADD MULTIPLES OF 10

Journey through the castle maze to rescue the dragon. Add
multiples of 10 to the 2-digit number to choose the correct answer.

ADDING A 2-DIGIT NUMBER THAT LEAPS ACROSS THE TENS

Shhh! Quietly tiptoe along the shelves to find a book to read. Add the 2-digit numbers together and follow the answers along the way.

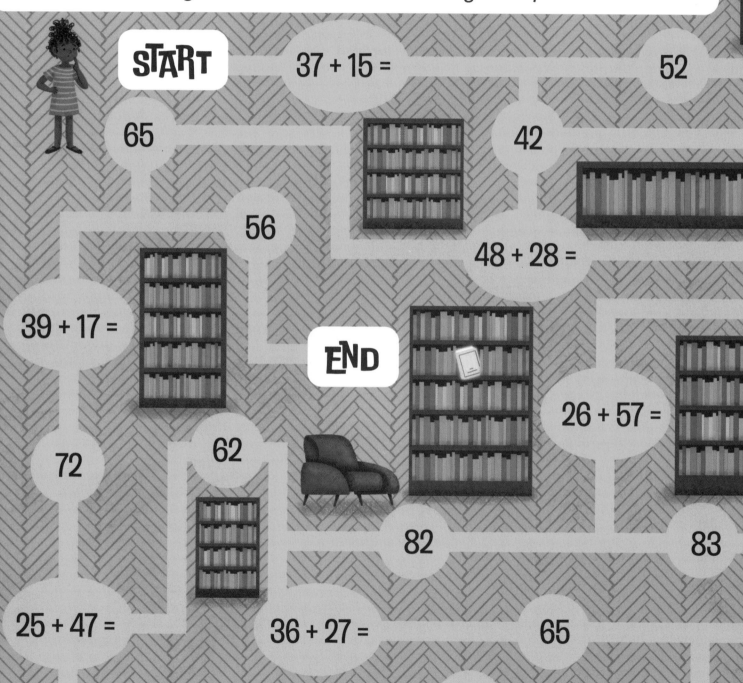

START

$37 + 15 =$

52

65

42

56

$48 + 28 =$

$39 + 17 =$

END

$26 + 57 =$

72

62

82

83

$25 + 47 =$

$36 + 27 =$

65

64

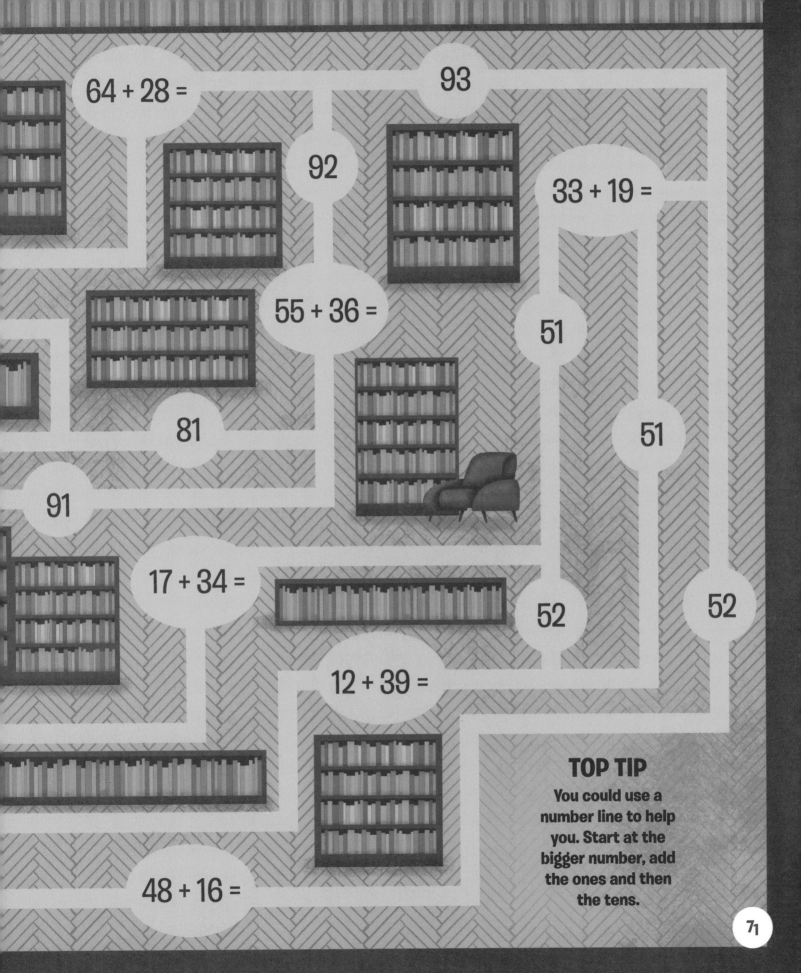

64 + 28 =

93

92

33 + 19 =

55 + 36 =

51

81

51

91

17 + 34 =

52

52

12 + 39 =

TOP TIP

You could use a
number line to help
you. Start at the
bigger number, add
the ones and then
the tens.

48 + 16 =

LET'S TRY ADDING 3 NUMBERS

Journey across the desert on a camel. Add the three numbers together to find the correct path.

$4 + 4 + 6 =$

15

14

18

17

$6 + 6 + 9 =$

$9 + 9 + 7 =$

$7 + 8 + 3 =$

26

25

TOP TIP

Look out for doubles or number bonds to ten. Remember you can add in any order.

$2 + 3 = 3 + 2$

15

16

END

$5 + 5 + 5 =$

22

23

START

13

9 + 1 + 5 =

14

8 + 3 + 2 =

7 + 3 + 3 =

16

17

15

9 + 2 + 2 =

12

21

6 + 9 + 6 =

22

6 + 6 + 9 =

8 + 8 + 7 =

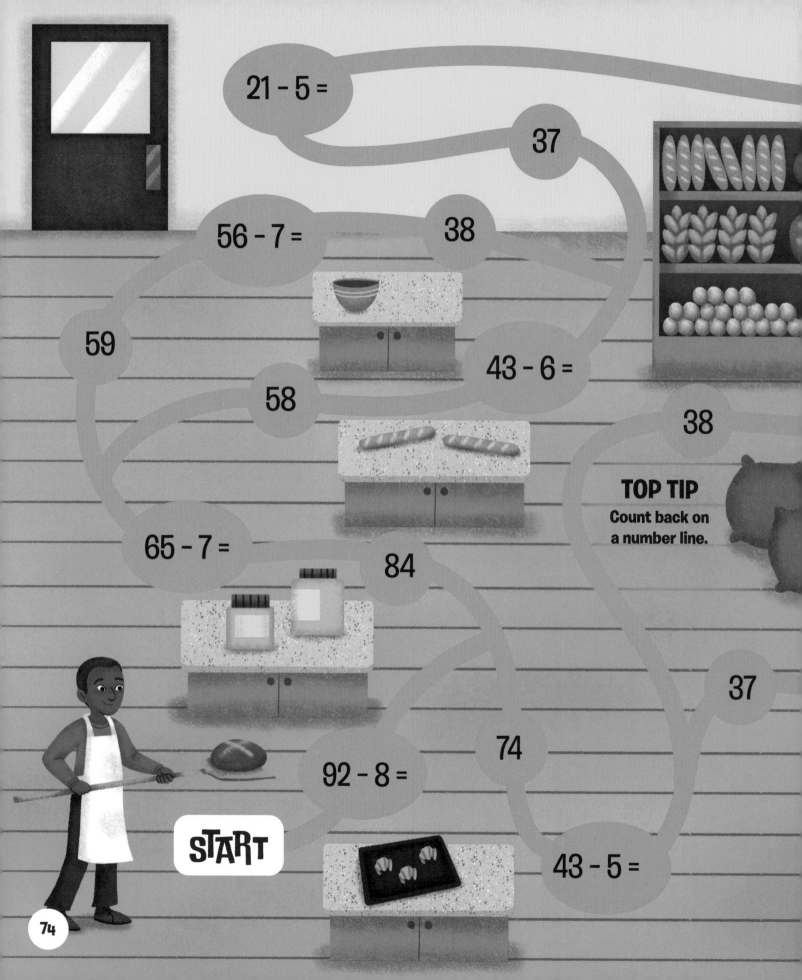

21 - 5 =

37

56 - 7 =

38

59

43 - 6 =

58

38

TOP TIP
Count back on
a number line.

65 - 7 =

84

37

92 - 8 =

74

START

43 - 5 =

74

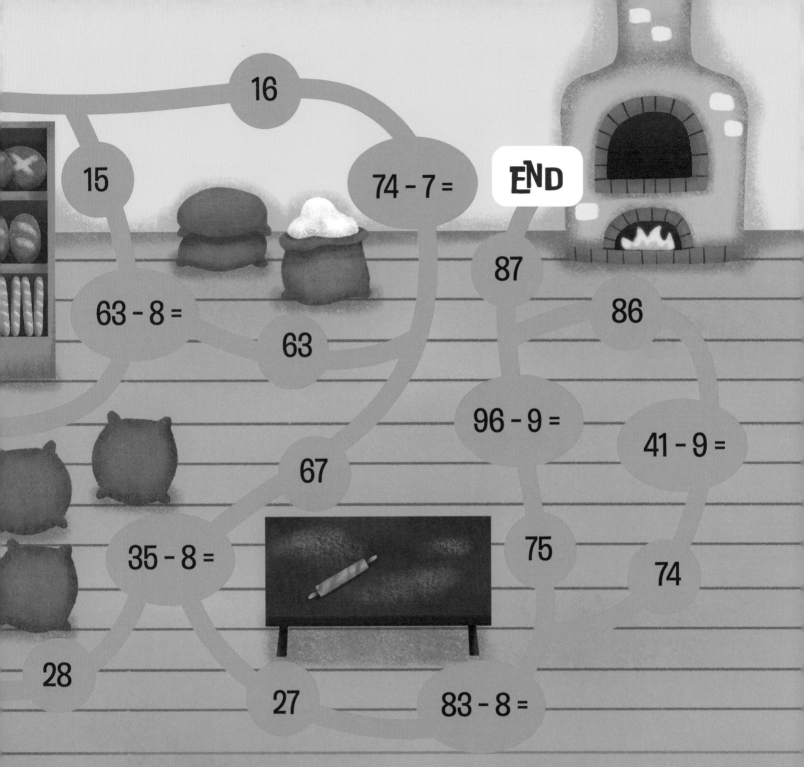

16

15

74 - 7 =

END

63 - 8 =

87

86

63

96 - 9 =

41 - 9 =

67

35 - 8 =

75

74

28

27

83 - 8 =

TAKE-AWAY A 1-DIGIT
NUMBER ACROSS THE TENS

The dough is ready to be baked. Guide the baker through the bakery to the ovens. Complete the subtraction problems to find the correct way.

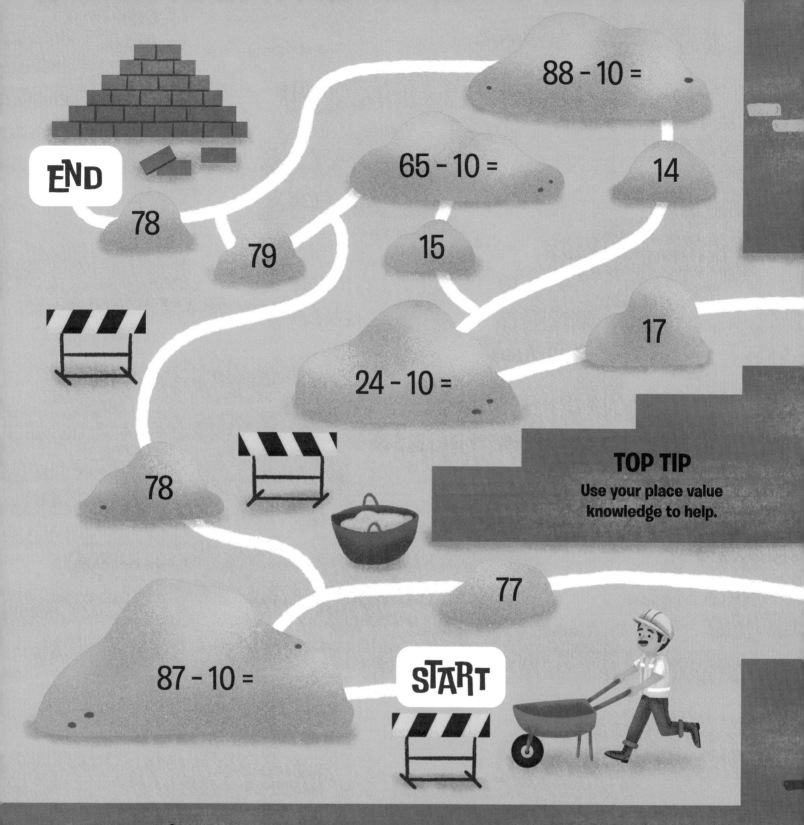

88 − 10 =

65 − 10 =

14

END

78

79

15

17

24 − 10 =

TOP TIP
Use your place value
knowledge to help.

78

77

87 − 10 =

START

TIME TO TAKE-AWAY TEN

Brick by brick the builder is building the wall. Take away 10 from each
number to guide the builder and his wheelbarrow to fetch more bricks.

27 - 10 =

53

73

63 - 10 =

65 - 10 =

18

81

71

47

46

38 - 10 =

91 - 10 =

28

39 - 10 =

29

56 - 10 =

START

100 - 20 =

80

100 - 70 =

90

100 - 70 =

40

30

30

TOP TIP
Use your number
bonds to help.
10 - 2 = 8
100 - 20 = 80

40

20

100 - 60 =

50

100 - 40 =

60

80

100 - 10 =

90

TAKE AWAY MULTIPLES OF TEN FROM 100

Float in this hot-air balloon to the landing field. Take-away multiples of ten to find the right route through the clouds.

100 - 50 =

50

40

100 - 60 =

100 - 80 =

100

100 - 0 =

100 - 100 =

0

100 - 10 =

100

30

0

100 - 60 =

40

END

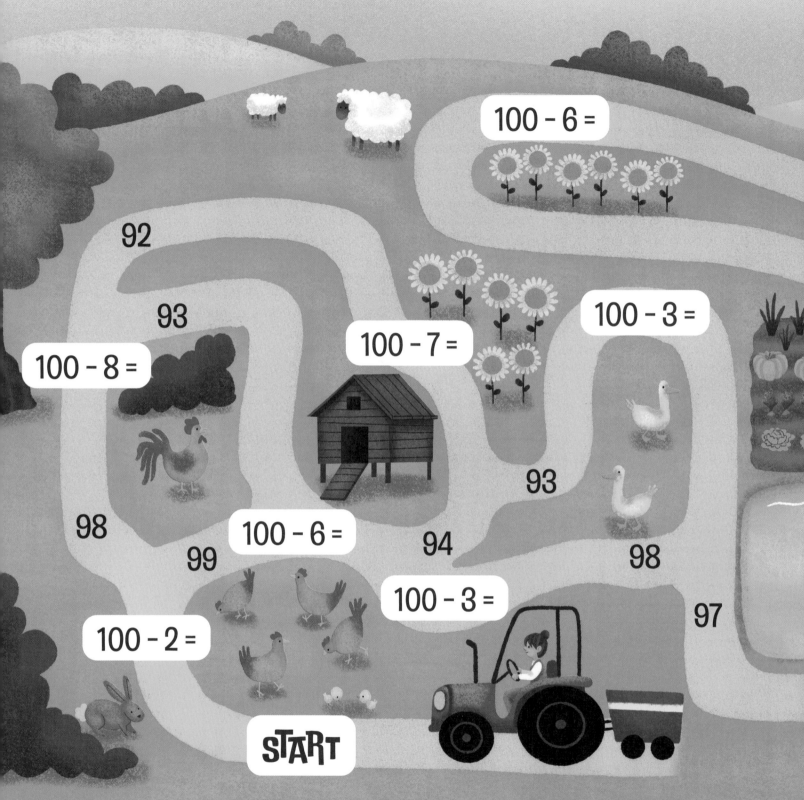

TAKe AWAY FROM 100

Take the tractor on its way through the farmyard to the hay barn. Solve the subtraction problems to find a route around the animals.

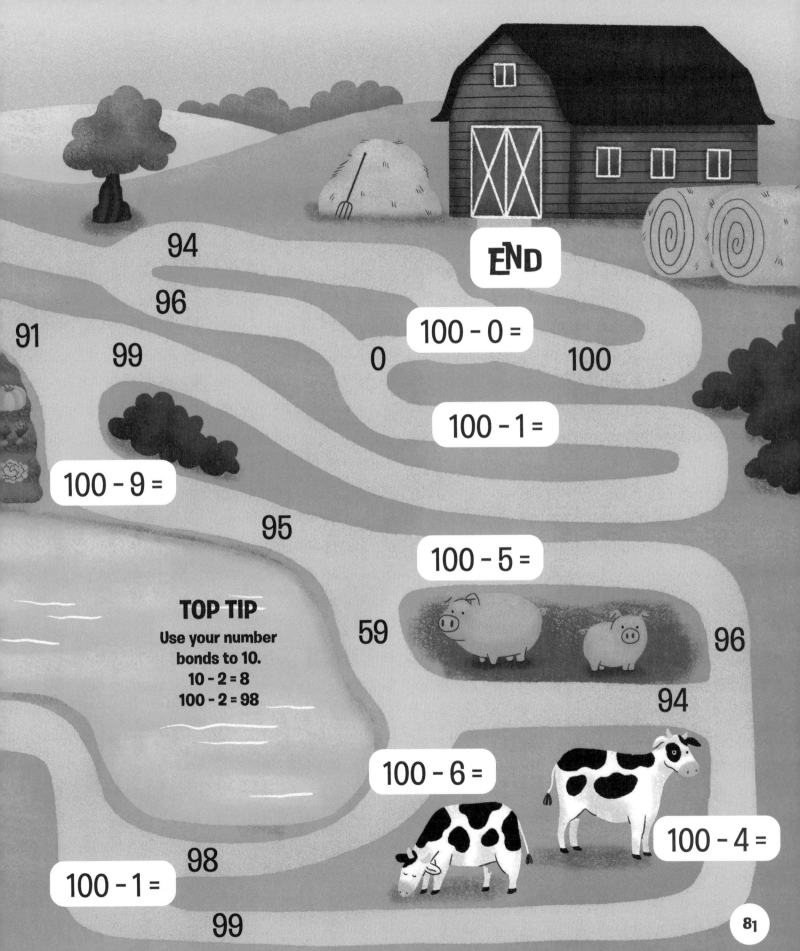

94

96

91

99

END

100 − 0 =

0   100

100 − 1 =

100 − 9 =

95

100 − 5 =

TOP TIP
Use your number
bonds to 10.
10 − 2 = 8
100 − 2 = 98

59

96

94

100 − 6 =

100 − 4 =

98

100 − 1 =

99

100 TAKE AWAY A 2-DIGIT NUMBER

Dive down deep with the diver to delve through the shipwreck. Subtract the numbers and follow the answers.

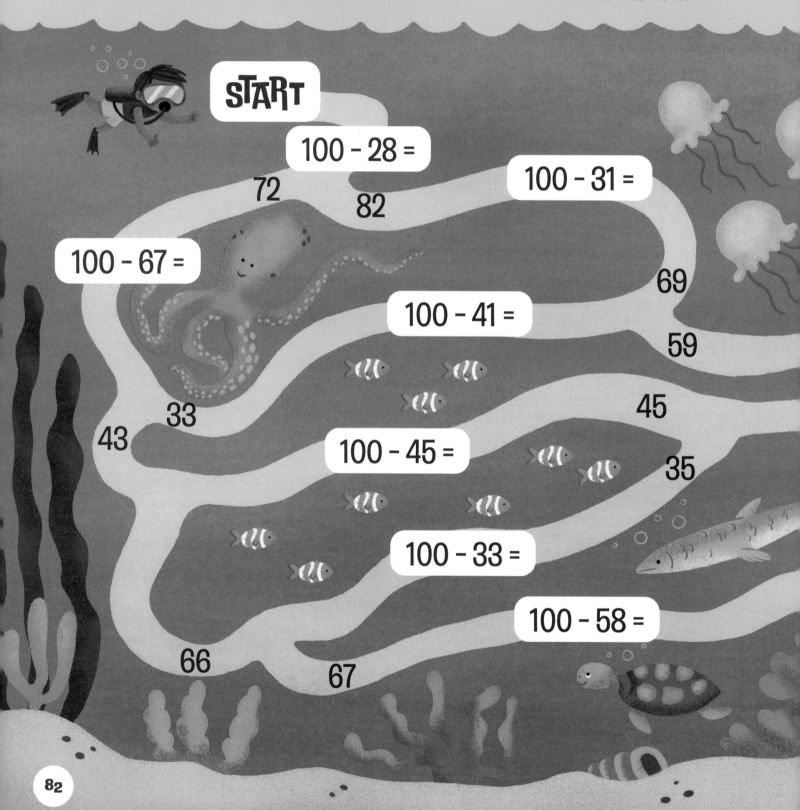

START

100 − 28 =

72

82

100 − 31 =

100 − 67 =

69

100 − 41 =

59

33

45

43

100 − 45 =

35

100 − 33 =

66

100 − 58 =

67

TOP TIP
Partition into tens and ones.
28 = 20 + 8
Take away the ones, then take away the tens.

100 − 25 =

75

85

100 − 15 =

59

100 − 51 =

49

100 − 65 =

100 − 23 =

42

76

100 − 19 =

52

77

100 − 17 =

83

END

93

83

MIXED ADDING AND SUBTRACTING TO 50

Guide the reindeer herder to his camp. Complete the problems to stay on the right path.

43

39 - 4 =

44

36 + 7 =

42

14 + 23 =

32

37

48 - 6 =

47

50 - 3 =

START

23 + 5 =

28

29

41

26 + 15 =

END

31

28

43 - 15 =

18

34

35

14 + 23 =

35

45

TOP TIP
Check the
operation. Is
it add or
take-away?

25 + 12 =

37

28 + 17 =

47

39 - 23 =

16

63 - 21 =

26

MIXED ADDING AND SUBTRACTING TO 100

Jump along with the kangaroo back to the joey. Add and subtract the numbers to find the correct path.

START

$80 - 3 =$

77

67

69

$6 + 43 =$

$63 + 5 =$

$95 - 47 =$

68

84

81

48

71

$64 + 17 =$

$7 + 59 =$

$61 - 12 =$

END

66

76

TOP TIP

These questions are mixed addition and subtraction.
Check the symbol—is it add or subtract?

87 - 4 =

83

84

58 + 5 =

43 - 11 =

73   63

96 - 2 =

6 + 43 =   95

94

65 - 23 =

42

98

41

75 + 23 =

88

54

93 - 24 =

ANSWERS

PAGES 4–5

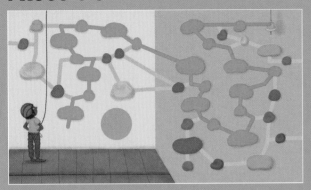

2 + 6 = 8   2 + 5 = 7   9 + 1 = 10
4 + 5 = 9   1 + 4 = 5   4 + 3 = 7
7 + 1 = 8   5 + 3 = 8
3 + 1 = 4   2 + 1 = 3

PAGES 6–7

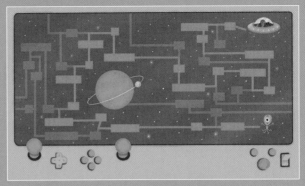

3 + 7 = 10   5 + 5 = 10   9 + 1 = 10
6 + 4 = 10   7 + 3 = 10   0 + 10 = 10
2 + 8 = 10   4 + 6 = 10
1 + 9 = 10   8 + 2 = 10

PAGES 8–9

10 − 3 = 7   10 − 4 = 6   10 − 0 = 10
10 − 6 = 4   10 − 8 = 2   10 − 7 = 3
10 − 2 = 8   10 − 9 = 1
10 − 1 = 9   10 − 5 = 5

PAGES 10–11

2 + 3 = 5   6 + 3 = 9   5 + 5 = 10
7 + 2 = 9   3 + 5 = 8   2 + 2 = 4
4 + 3 = 7   7 + 1 = 8
5 + 3 = 8   4 + 5 = 9

PAGES 12–13

0 + 10 = 10   4 + 10 = 14   8 + 10 = 18
5 + 10 = 15   6 + 10 = 16   2 + 10 = 12
10 + 10 = 20   9 + 10 = 19
3 + 10 = 13   7 + 10 = 17

PAGES 14–15

15 + 2 = 17   13 + 2 = 15   2 + 12 = 14
7 + 5 = 12   8 + 11 = 19   16 + 3 = 19
6 + 8 = 14   5 + 13 = 18
12 + 6 = 18   4 + 9 = 13

PAGES 16–17

12 + 8 = 20   18 + 2 = 20   7 + 13 = 20
17 + 3 = 20   15 + 5 = 20   10 + 10 = 20
16 + 4 = 20   1 + 19 = 20
11 + 9 = 20   6 + 14 = 20

PAGES 18–19

20 − 3 = 17   20 − 2 = 18   20 − 7 = 13
20 − 1 = 19   20 − 5 = 15   20 − 0 = 20
20 − 6 = 14   20 − 4 = 16
20 − 9 = 11   20 − 8 = 12

PAGES 20–21

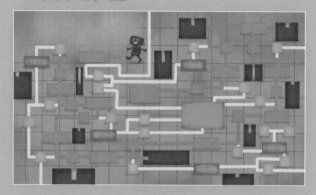

16 − 4 = 12   13 − 7 = 6   11 − 8 = 3
17 − 5 = 12   18 − 6 = 12   20 − 6 = 14
12 − 8 = 4   19 − 9 = 10
15 − 5 = 10   14 − 3 = 11

PAGES 22–23

3 + 3 = 6   8 + 8 = 16   1 + 1 = 2
5 + 5 = 10   10 + 10 = 20   6 + 6 = 12
2 + 2 = 4   7 + 7 = 14

PAGES 24–25

11 + 11 = 22   14 + 14 = 28   17 + 17 = 34
12 + 12 = 24   15 + 15 = 30   18 + 18 = 36
13 + 13 = 26   16 + 16 = 32   19 + 19 = 38

PAGES 26–27

23 + 4 = 27   33 + 4 = 37   5 + 34 = 39
6 + 32 = 38   44 + 3 = 47   8 + 21 = 29
41 + 5 = 46   2 + 26 = 28   1 + 46 = 47

PAGES 28-29

20 + 30 = 50	60 + 20 = 80	60 + 10 = 70
10 + 30 = 40	40 + 10 = 50	30 + 40 = 70
40 + 20 = 60	70 + 20 = 90	
80 + 10 = 90	50 + 30 = 80	

PAGES 30-31

18 + 10 = 28	23 + 10 = 33	37 + 10 = 47
27 + 10 = 37	56 + 10 = 66	89 + 10 = 99
71 + 10 = 81	32 + 10 = 42	
44 + 10 = 54	64 + 10 = 74	

PAGES 32-33

28 + 20 = 48	66 + 20 = 86	46 + 10 = 56
35 + 40 = 75	34 + 50 = 84	17 + 40 = 57
13 + 30 = 43	24 + 20 = 44	
47 + 50 = 97	39 + 20 = 59	

PAGES 34-35

64 + 12 = 76	56 + 21 = 77	43 + 41 = 84
52 + 17 = 69	41 + 32 = 73	35 + 21 = 56
33 + 55 = 88	64 + 21 = 85	
22 + 47 = 69	35 + 22 = 57	

PAGES 36-37

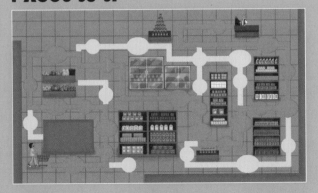

1 + 3 + 7 = 11	9 + 4 + 1 = 14	4 + 7 + 6 = 17
5 + 5 + 3 = 13	3 + 4 + 6 = 13	4 + 5 + 5 = 14
2 + 8 + 6 = 16	8 + 8 + 3 = 19	8 + 5 + 2 = 15

PAGES 38-39

86 - 3 = 83	87 - 6 = 81	56 - 5 = 51
79 - 2 = 77	97 - 5 = 92	43 - 2 = 41
46 - 1 = 45	77 - 7 = 70	
54 - 3 = 51	38 - 3 = 35	

PAGES 40-41

56 − 10 = 46
82 − 10 = 72
64 − 10 = 54

31 − 10 = 21
47 − 10 = 37
28 − 10 = 18

73 − 10 = 63
18 − 10 = 8

PAGES 42-43

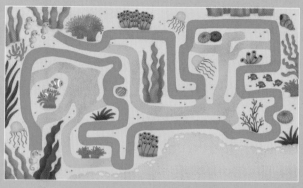

71 − 20 = 51
83 − 40 = 43
69 − 20 = 49
52 − 30 = 22

94 − 50 = 44
47 − 30 = 17
36 − 20 = 16
86 − 60 = 26

72 − 60 = 12
57 − 20 = 37

PAGES 44-45

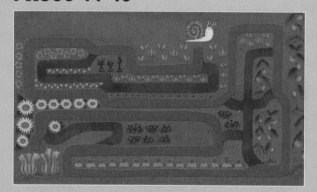

59 − 32 = 27
72 − 41 = 31
58 − 13 = 45
46 − 25 = 21

67 − 42 = 25
85 − 63 = 22
96 − 65 = 31
55 − 21 = 34

39 − 12 = 27
27 − 16 = 11

PAGES 46-47

20 + 20 = 40
21 + 21 = 42
22 + 22 = 44
23 + 23 = 46

24 + 24 = 48
25 + 25 = 50
26 + 26 = 52
27 + 27 = 54

28 + 28 = 56
29 + 29 = 58

PAGES 48-49

10 + 10 = 20
15 + 15 = 30
20 + 20 = 40

25 + 25 = 50
30 + 30 = 60
35 + 35 = 70

40 + 40 = 80
45 + 45 = 90
50 + 50 = 100

PAGES 50-51

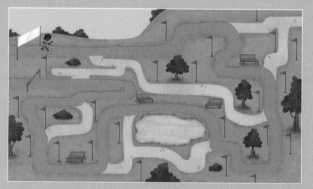

10 + 10 = 20
20 + 20 = 40
30 + 30 = 60
40 + 40 = 80

50 + 50 = 100
60 + 60 = 120
70 + 70 = 140
80 + 80 = 160

90 + 90 = 180
100 + 100 = 200

PAGES 52-53

10 + 20 + 30 = 60   80 + 40 + 20 = 140   30 + 40 + 30 = 100
40 + 60 + 10 = 110   20 + 80 + 50 = 150   70 + 50 + 30 = 150
50 + 50 + 20 = 120   70 + 30 + 30 = 130
90 + 30 + 10 = 130   40 + 40 + 20 = 100

PAGES 54-55

27 - 10 = 17   36 + 20 = 56   48 + 20 = 68
45 + 20 = 65   82 - 50 = 32   83 - 40 = 43
76 - 30 = 46   97 - 80 = 17
15 + 40 = 55   61 - 30 = 31

PAGES 56-57

28 + 1 = 29   52 + 1 = 53   61 + 1 = 62
76 + 1 = 77   37 + 1 = 38   84 + 1 = 85
43 + 1 = 44   13 + 1 = 14   95 + 1 = 96

PAGES 58-59

28 - 1 = 27   52 - 1 = 51   61 - 1 = 60
76 - 1 = 75   37 - 1 = 36   84 - 1 = 83
43 - 1 = 42   13 - 1 = 12

PAGES 60-61

9 + 1 = 10   39 + 1 = 40   69 + 1 = 70
19 + 1 = 20   49 + 1 = 50   79 + 1 = 80
29 + 1 = 30   59 + 1 = 60   89 + 1 = 90

PAGES 62-63

100 - 1 = 99   70 - 1 = 69   40 - 1 = 39
90 - 1 = 89   60 - 1 = 59   30 - 1 = 29
80 - 1 = 79   50 - 1 = 49   20 - 1 - 19

PAGES 64–65

5 + 26 = 31	7 + 46 = 53	9 + 52 = 61
6 + 55 = 61	3 + 79 = 82	2 + 88 = 90
8 + 34 = 42	4 + 28 = 32	7 + 65 = 72

PAGES 66–67

100 + 23 = 123	100 + 37 = 137	100 + 12 = 112
100 + 82 = 182	100 + 45 = 145	100 + 56 = 156
100 + 74 = 174	100 + 61 = 161	

PAGES 68–69

10 + 28 = 38	70 + 29 = 99	20 + 35 = 55
50 + 37 = 87	80 + 13 = 93	40 + 22 = 62
30 + 65 = 95	60 + 14 = 74	30 + 23 = 53

PAGES 70–71

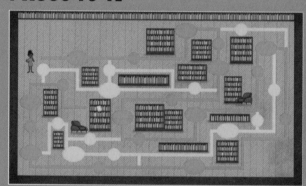

37 + 15 = 52	26 + 57 = 83	48 + 16 = 64
64 + 28 = 92	17 + 34 = 51	25 + 47 = 72
55 + 36 = 91	33 + 19 = 52	39 + 17 = 56

PAGES 72–73

8 + 3 + 2 = 13	4 + 4 + 6 = 14	8 + 8 + 7 = 23
9 + 1 + 5 = 15	9 + 9 + 7 = 25	5 + 5 + 5 = 15
7 + 8 + 3 = 18	6 + 9 + 6 = 21	

PAGES 74–75

92 − 8 = 84	21 − 5 = 16	83 − 8 = 75
65 − 7 = 58	74 − 7 = 67	96 − 9 = 87
43 − 6 = 37	35 − 8 = 27	

PAGES 76-77

87 - 10 = 77   91 - 10 = 81   24 - 10 = 14
39 - 10 = 29   63 - 10 = 53   88 - 10 = 78
56 - 10 = 46   27 - 10 = 17

PAGES 78-79

100 - 20 = 80   100 - 70 = 30   100 - 0 = 100
100 - 50 = 50   100 - 40 = 60   100 - 100 = 0
100 - 80 = 20   100 - 10 = 90   100 - 60 = 40

PAGES 80-81

100 - 2 = 98   100 - 1 = 99   100 - 6 = 94
100 - 8 = 92   100 - 4 = 96   100 - 0 = 100
100 - 7 = 93   100 - 5 = 95
100 - 3 = 97   100 - 9 = 91

PAGES 82-83

100 - 28 = 72   100 - 51 = 49   100 - 23 = 77
100 - 67 = 33   100 - 65 = 35   100 - 17 = 83
100 - 41 = 59   100 - 33 = 67
100 - 25 = 75   100 - 58 = 42

PAGES 84-85

50 - 3 = 47   39 - 4 = 35   43 - 15 = 28
23 + 5 = 28   25 + 12 = 37   26 + 15 = 41
48 - 6 = 42   39 - 23 = 16
36 + 7 = 43   28 + 17 = 45

PAGES 86-87

80 - 3 = 77   96 - 2 = 94   95 - 47 = 48
63 + 5 = 68   75 + 23 = 98   7 + 59 = 66
87 - 4 = 83   65 - 23 = 42
58 + 5 = 63   64 + 17 = 81

Resources

Hundred square

1	2	3	4	5	6	7	8	9	10
11	12	13	14	15	16	17	18	19	20
21	22	23	24	25	26	27	28	29	30
31	32	33	34	35	36	37	38	39	40
41	42	43	44	45	46	47	48	49	50
51	52	53	54	55	56	57	58	59	60
61	62	63	64	65	66	67	68	69	70
71	72	73	74	75	76	77	78	79	80
81	82	83	84	85	86	87	88	89	90
91	92	93	94	95	96	97	98	99	100

Number line

1	2	3	4	5	6	7	8	9	10	11	12	13	14	15	16	17	18	19	20